DREAM OF EMPIRE

FRANZ HUBMANN

DREAM OF EMPIRE

THE WORLD OF GERMANY IN ORIGINAL PHOTOGRAPHS 1840–1914

EDITED BY J. M. WHEATCROFT

LONDON
ROUTLEDGE & KEGAN PAUL

COPYRIGHT © 1972 BY VERLAG FRITZ MOLDEN, WIEN-MÜNCHEN-ZÜRICH
FIRST PUBLISHED IN 1972 AS
DAS DEUTSCHE FAMILIENALBUM: DIE WELT VON GESTERN
IN ALTEN PHOTOGRAPHIEN
FIRST PUBLISHED IN GREAT BRITAIN IN 1973
BY ROUTLEDGE & KEGAN PAUL LTD
BROADWAY HOUSE, 68-74 CARTER LANE
LONDON EC4V 5EL
© ROUTLEDGE & KEGAN PAUL 1973
ALL RIGHTS RESERVED. NO PART OF THIS BOOK MAY BE REPRODUCED
IN ANY FORM WITHOUT PERMISSION FROM THE PUBLISHER AND THE
PROPRIETOR OF THE ORIGINAL COPYRIGHT, EXCEPT FOR THE
QUOTATION OF BRIEF PASSAGES IN CRITICISM
JACKET AND LAYOUT: HANS SCHAUMBERGER, VIENNA
PRINTED IN AUSTRIA BY G. GISTEL & CIE, VIENNA
TYPE: GARAMOND-ANTIQUA
BINDING: ALBERT GÜNTHER, VIENNA
ISBN 0 7100 7587 1

CONTENTS

INTRODUCTION

In the cold dawn of Sunday, November 10, 1918, a convoy of cars arrived at the Dutch border-post of Eÿsden, near Maastricht. A small group of German officers left the cars and crossed the Dutch frontier on foot; in this subdued, almost furtive, manner, Wilhelm II, German Emperor, left his dominions for the last time. It was the start of an exile that was to last until his death at Doorn in 1941. The Empire, which had been so theatrically proclaimed forty-seven years before in the Hall of Mirrors at Versailles, in the presence of all the notables of Germany, ended amidst chaos and revolution. The Emperor's departure aroused mixed feelings. Many in Germany felt he had deserted his post and that, "like a German hero of old, the Emperor should have proceeded to the front, charged the enemy at the head of a detachment and sought death in a final attack." Others, more cruelly, made remarks to the effect that nothing became him more in his thirty years' reign than leaving it. In these two differing reactions, one the product of romantic notions of the German past, the other of a cynical, hard-hearted practicality, can be seen two of the many conflicting elements which manifested themselves in the German Empire. This book records the images of the Empire, but this short introduction is intended to indicate what lay behind them.

For many Germans, the creation of a truly German Empire had been a dream since early youth. Before 1806 when Napoleon had abolished the Holy Roman Empire, Germany had consisted of over three hundred states, some of which covered only a few square miles. For administrative purposes, he had reduced this number to thirty, and when the Congress of Vienna had set about re-establishing something of the old order, it had established a German Confederation of thirty-nine sovereign states. But the bitter experience of the Napoleonic wars, and France's years of triumph, had shown Germans the power of a strong united state, and even those conservatives who hated the French Revolution with its radical social doctrines, admired, in spite of themselves, the power and purpose of Napoleon's empire. But in the period between 1815 and 1848, Germany outwardly slumbered, though beneath the surface dissatisfaction mounted against the rigid and repressive systems manipulated by the Austrian Chancellor, Metternich. The Revolution of 1848, which spread from Paris to convulse most of Europe, was the first real opportunity for the middle classes in Germany to break free from the traditional and often autocratic governments under which they lived. The revolution took a different form in each state, sometimes peaceful, sometimes the product of considerable violence. At first, the revolutionaries had many purely local grievances, but common, national aims soon emerged. They looked forward to a united Germany in which freedom could flourish; one student expressed the hopes of many when he wrote: "I was dominated by a feeling that at last the great opportunity had arrived for giving to the German people the liberty which was their birthright and to the German fatherland, unity and greatness." In the heady days of spring and summer 1848, it seemed as though revolution was going to succeed. Constitutions were scattered like confetti, the King of Prussia, fearing for his throne, appeared in the streets of Berlin sporting the black red gold colours of the Revolution, and solid, middle-class delegates—like those on pages 70 and 71—were elected to a National Assembly which was to sit in the old Imperial town of Frankfurt on Main. On May 18 three hundred and thirty delegates from all parts of Germany marched in triumphant and solemn procession across the Römerberg in Frankfurt (see pages 67, 72, 73) to St. Paul's Church, where the National Assembly was to meet. But their elation was misplaced, for the middle classes still had no real power. What had caused the *ancien régime* to collapse in the face of pressure was not so much the threat from the middle classes, as the danger of a much more serious revolution from the peasants and artisans. All over Germany sporadic outbreaks of violence had occurred, and the authorities (the French Revolution of less than sixty years before never far from their minds) had given in too easily. As time went on, however, they realised that the initiative still lay with them and in state after state, the old order was gradually restored. In the meantime, the delegates at Frankfurt decided, after much deliberation, to offer the Imperial throne of a constitutional Germany to the King of Prussia. He, too, had recovered from his panic of March 1848 and spurned the crown, calling it in private, "a diadem moulded out of the dirt and dregs of revolution, disloyalty and treason". Revolution crumbled all over Europe, and the National Assembly of Germany, finding no taker for its crown, and having no means to maintain itself in power, slowly dispersed. The first attempt to fulfil the dream of a united Germany had collapsed.

Although the attempt to create the Empire from below had failed, the desire for it had not abated. Prince Albert, German Consort of Queen Victoria, typified the passion for unity which gripped Germany. With characteristic logic and clearheadedness, he planned and schemed for the unification of Germany under the leadership of a reformed Prussia, which he believed the only force in Germany capable of holding together a fledgling Empire. In pursuit of his policy, he set up the marriage of his eldest daughter Vicky to the eventual heir to the Prussian throne, hoping thereby to temper the authoritarian tradition of Prussia with the more liberal attitudes of the smaller German states, of which he was a product. Far from being a mere pawn, Vicky had inherited much of her father's incisive intellect, and totally embraced his views, whilst her fiancé, Prince Friedrich Wilhelm, hero-worshipped the prince, and spent many hours of indoctrination during visits to Windsor or Balmoral. Prince Albert's plans did not lack support in his homeland. Many men of the time, particularly those who could remember Germany's disgrace at the hands of Napoleon, firmly believed that only through unity could Germany take up its proper place in the world. In the twenty years following the revolution of 1848, the urge towards Empire strengthened still further as its enthusiasts passionately propagandised their cause. Pressure groups were founded, like the National Union of 1859, as well as hundreds of smaller clubs, patriotic societies, and groups for the study of German culture. They sprang up all over Germany, and seemingly innocent events, like artists' discussion groups (page 127) or choral festivals (page 166) became vehicles for the nationalist cause. Slowly, these many groups came together in support of a common programme, which accepted, albeit reluctantly in many cases, that Prussia must stand at the head of the new Germany.

The Empire, when it came, did so, not as the men of 1848 had hoped, through the ballot box, as the product of reason and debate, but as the direct result of war. On July 3, 1866, after a campaign marked by strategic daring and skill of execution on the Prussian side, a decisive battle was fought at Königgrätz in Bohemia, between the two contenders for power in Germany, Austria and Prussia. As a result of her defeat, Austria was forced out of the German confederation, and Prussia was left as the most powerful force in Germany. Her military strength was again demonstrated to the rest of the world when, just over four years later, on July 17, 1870, the French were manoeuvred into declaring war on Prussia. The same strategic genius which the Prussian Chief of Staff, Helmut von Moltke (page 192) had shown in 1866 once more came into play. Using several armies simultaneously, and attacking swiftly, he upset the balance of the French defence. By the end of August, the French armies, believed by many informed military experts to be the best in Europe, were in disarray. On September 2, 1870, the French Emperor, Napoleon III, surrendered, and a Republic was proclaimed in France. The ex-emperor was sent into temporary captivity in Germany, and, on his release, found his way to England, where he died shortly afterwards. The radicals took control in Paris which held out staunchly, and in conditions of immense hardship, until the end of January 1871. The stunning victories in the field prepared the way for the foundation of a German Empire. The war had been engineered by Prussia, and controlled by Prussia, but it was seen as a *German* victory for all the states of the Confederation had contributed money or troops. Indeed, some of the smaller states who had sided with Austria in the war of 1866 particularly distinguished themselves in the war against France, and it was from this sense of united victory that the Empire, proclaimed four months later, sprang.

THE CREATION OF IMPERIAL GERMANY

The Empire, long expected, was now a reality and it aroused a variety of emotions. To the ardently romantic nationalist, it was a supreme triumph. The historian Heinrich von Sybel wrote: "How have I earned so much of God's favour as to be allowed to live through such a great and mighty experience? And how shall I go on living? What has for twenty years been the substance of every wish and every aspiration is now realised in such an infinitely magnificent way." Another school of thought saw the Empire as a natural fulfilment of the German past: "The re-awakening of the Emperor Barbarossa has been a dream in the imagination of our people and the theme of the songs of our poets. And lo, dreams and fantasies, songs and sayings, hopes and aspirations, have suddenly found fulfilment in a wholly unexpected way... With the new German Empire we have renewed our contact with memories of Germany's past." But others, particularly in the south of Germany, feared the harsh domination of Prussia, which, in the ardour of victory, might sweep aside all constitutional safeguards: "It is bondage, the opposite of popular self determination, that has brought about the foundation of this Empire." Distaste was expressed in another, and perhaps more surprising quarter—none other than the new Emperor himself. King Wilhelm I, who now became, at the age of seventy-four, Emperor Wilhelm I, spoke for all the traditional forces in Prussia when he denounced the new creation as a "Shadow Empire", looking upon his newly exalted position as a cross which he had, unwillingly, to bear. On the eve of his proclamation, he told the Prussian State Council that "he could not describe to us all how desperate he felt at having to take leave tomorrow of the old Prussia to which he alone held steadfast, and wished to hold steadfast in the future. Sobs and tears interrupted his words..." He expressed similar sentiments even more vehemently in his letters to his wife from France.

These doubts and hesitations on all sides indicate how fundamentally disunited was the new Empire. Despite all the emotional pressures in its favour, it was bitterly resented when it finally took shape. The responsibility for its creation and structure was almost exclusively that of one man—Otto von Bismarck-Schönhausen—who had forced it into being by his great skill and ingenuity. The Empire he created had one prime function: the dominance of Prussia in Germany. He wrote: "The form in which the King of Prussia exercises his rule in Germany was never of special importance to me. But I have put the whole strength that God has given me to the effective establishment of this Rule." The new Imperial Crown was offered, not by the people, but by the princes and rulers of the German states, and they accepted a federal structure which allowed them autonomy in very many issues, but which conserved the real power in the hands of the Emperor (who could only be the King of Prussia). This federal state was equipped with all the trappings of constitutional government, with a Reichstag, elected by universal suffrage of all males over twenty-one, and a Bundesrat, which represented every state of the new Empire. But the new arrangements did little to alter the traditional position of the King of Prussia, and in every important respect the Prussian system remained intact. There was no Imperial Army, because the new Emperor had refused to inflict what he considered to be an indignity on his loyal Prussian soldiers, but he had proved willing to accept an Imperial Navy, a decision of crucial importance. In the long-term interests of Prussia, the constitution was a brilliant success. Some claimed it to be Bismarck's masterpiece, although the bulk of the conservative Prussian aristocracy considered it to have gone too far in the direction of Democracy and Revolution.

Bismarck's political thinking was based on cynicism. With one hand he granted the vote on a wide basis, and with the other arranged a Reichstag in which the deputies elected should have limited powers. In this respect it proved to be the Shadow Empire which the Emperor had prophesied, since most of its structure was superfluous, serving no other function than to conceal the real seat of power, and to bolster the pride and prestige of those who participated in it. The minor states might rejoice at their independence, the deputies might debate and vote, the electorate might express its will, but all to little or no effect. This is not to say that the machinery always worked to Bismarck's order, and that the Reichstag always followed the Government's lead. Indeed, the iron will of Bismarck was needed to make the constitution work to the best effect, and the rise of new political forces, such as social democracy, could easily upset the balance; but they could not alter the basic character of the Empire, in which power, in the last analysis, resided firmly and exclusively in the hands of the Emperor and his ministers.

BLOOD AND IRON

The first quarter-century of the Empire was dominated by the personality of Bismarck (pages 202, 250, 252), and bore his stamp indelibly. Almost single-handedly, he ensured and reinforced the position of Germany in European politics by weaving a web of intricate diplomacy, with Germany at its centre. At the same time he clipped the wings of opposition groups within, denouncing them publicly as enemies of the Empire. By his harsh and unaccommodating approach to politics, he gave to German affairs that tone of brutalism which so quickly became apparent to foreigners, even though they might admire the clean streets, industrial achievements, and fine cultural life of the new state. Indeed so closely had the man become identified with the state, that Germany without Bismarck seemed a near impossibility, and when, in 1890, he was forced to resign by a young and confident Wilhelm II, the shock both at home and abroad, was immense. That most famous of Punch cartoons "Dropping the Pilot" was part of the wave of disbelief in Britain. The Iron Chancellor did not yield gracefully, and from his home at Friedrichsruh, near Hamburg, he waged a guerrilla war against his successors almost until his death in 1898. But though his shadow still hung over politics, his withdrawal from power nevertheless marked something of a turning-point. As the great historian, Friedrich Meinecke, remarked, "in all of Germany something new can be detected about 1890, politically, and intellectually as well..."

The cynicism and harshness of Bismarck's Germany was hated by those whose concept of society was more romantic. They looked for a new culture and ideology which owed little to the traditional, brutal Prussianism which Bismarck characterised. Some thought that they had found their inspiration in the new Emperor, Wilhelm II, whose self-assured flamboyant character, as well as his youth, had much appeal. They believed that Germany needed a leader, who would "set the dead masses in motion" (Julius Langbehn). A generation of young Germans waxed their moustaches in imitation of the unmistakable and idiosyncratic Imperial model, and indulged in demonstrations of exaggerated nationalism. They flocked to the loyalist societies, like the All Deutsche Verband or the Navy League, and, joined by many of their elders, formed a patriotic caucus in German society. By 1914, over half of the population of Germany was under the age of fifteen, an appropriate statistic for the country which, above all others, venerated the energy and idealism of youth.

The instrument which transformed the "Shadow Empire" into a world power was the explosive growth of Germany's trade and industry after 1871. The industrialist Paul Rohrbach, writing in the journal *Jugend* in 1912, commented shrewdly on the previous forty years: "Germany's rise has been favoured by the fact that the political and economic union of Germany coincided with the most wonderful technical progress that humanity had ever seen. And this technique, founded on the methodical knowledge of nature, corresponded exactly in a most brilliant manner with one of the traits of our national temperament—exact and laborious energy." During these forty years the character of Germany was transformed, physically and socially. In 1871, it was still a predominantly rural society, with almost two-thirds of the population living off the land: by 1910 the figure had shrunk to 40%. In that same period of just under forty years, the size of the larger cities increased dramatically—Berlin from 775,000 in 1870 to two million in 1910, Hamburg from 309,000 to 950,000 over the same years; by the end of the first decade of the twentieth century, almost six million of the population lived in cities of over half a million people. The magnet which drew them to urban life was the traditional hope for streets paved with gold, and the more tangible and realistic prospects of higher living standards. Despite the depression in world trade which began in the mid-seventies, and lasted to the mid-nineties, German industry and commerce grew steadily, shedding outmoded systems of production, and driving inefficient concerns into bankruptcy. Between 1870 and 1890 German industrial production grew about 20% in each five year period, but between 1891 and 1895 the rate doubled. By comparison, Britain, in these same five years, grew by only 15%, and the world figure (including Germany) was 26%. These increases in productivity meant greater prosperity spread throughout German society, and a growing confidence in the nation's ability to compete with the rest of the world.

Many Germans in positions of influence began to sense that this burgeoning economic power was not accompanied by a corresponding increase in influence in the international political sphere. Economic and social arguments were produced to demand a new status for Germany in the world. The economist Gustav Schmoller stated them succinctly in a newspaper article of May 1899: "We are the fastest growing nation in the world . . . if 52 million Germans continue to increase in the future as in the past, at the rate of 1 per cent per annum, by 1950 we shall have over 104 million Germans. How are we to feed these people in the homeland?... Proletarian conditions and pressure on wage levels of the worst kind must result if we do not summon up the energy to expand..." It began to be accepted, first among advanced thinkers, and then by the bulk of the upper classes, that Germany had to find new fields for her "exact and laborious energy". Bernhard von Bülow summarised the new feeling in a famous speech to the Reichstag in December 1897: "We do not by any means feel the need to stick our fingers in every pie, but on the other hand... the days when the German happily surrendered the land to one of his neighbours, to another, the sea, and reserved for himself the heavens, where pure doctrine was enthroned... (Laughter–Bravo!)... Those days are over... In a word, we don't want to put anyone in the shade, but we too demand our place in the sun." The claim had been staked.

"A PLACE IN THE SUN..."

The pictures in this volume are drawn from every corner of the German Empire, from Königsberg, on the Baltic, now the Russian town of Kaliningrad, to the great cities of the south, like Munich and Stuttgart. Snapshots record, impartially, destitute labourers from the east (page 315) and the cream of Imperial society (pages 260 to 264). But what the camera does not record are the hidden antagonisms which divided German society, possibly more so than any other country in Western Europe. Hatred and suspicion were rife. The catholic-dominated south disliked and feared the protestant-dominated north. The middle classes were apprehensive of the increasing power of the workers, whilst the aristocracy resented the intrusion of the bourgeoisie into the army and senior positions of State. Although all western European countries in the last half-century before the First World War shared some of these problems, few were so prone to self-doubt. The other major powers had what Germany lacked, a fixed traditional position in the world, and a clear sense of national identity. The new Germany believed that it had to fight for its rightful place; Wilhelm II, with characteristic public bombast, peppered his speeches with allusions to Germany's right to a world role. At the launching of the battleship *Wittelsbach* in July 1900 he declared, "I am not a man who believes that we Germans bled and conquered thirty years ago... in order to be pushed to one side when great international decisions call to be made. If that were to happen, the place of Germany as a world power would be gone for ever, and I am not prepared to let that happen. It is my duty and privilege to employ to this end without hesitation the most appropriate and, if need be, the sharpest methods." Not surprisingly, in this atmosphere of tension, a belief grew that Germany must struggle in every sphere—in commerce, in the arts, and in intellectual pursuits. From this need to struggle came the belief, partly a defence against the threat from outside, that German *Kultur* was superior to all others, and deserved not merely an equal but a dominant position in the world. The manifesto of the Pan-German League declared, "We believe that in working for the preservation and expansion of the German spirit in the world our people most effectively promote the construction of world morality. For our German *Kultur* represents the ideal core of the human intellect, and every step which is taken for Germanism belongs therefore to humanity as such and the future of our species." (1891) The old faith in the power of reason, strong in the Germany of 1848, was weakened, and between 1871 and 1914, German nationalism acquired a new tinge. The explorations by historians and folklorists, like the Brothers Grimm, into the world of the Germanic past had created a new culture in which all Germans could share.

It was a combination of myth, legend, and history; and it was this common past which made many people aware and proud of the fact that they were *Germans*, rather than Prussians, Saxons or Bavarians. A shared heritage made the traditional parochial disputes seem pointless, and to work together for the greater glory of the German state and nation was the logical consequence.

There were exceptions to the new consensus. At the two opposite poles of society—the old aristocracy and the working class—the Empire aroused less enthusiasm. German nationalism, in 1898 as in 1848, was largely a middle-class affair. To the gentry and nobility of Germany, and most especially that of Prussia, nationalism was still somehow equated with subversion. But Prussia, as the dominant force in the new Germany, had a great deal to gain from accepting the new spirit of the nation and in practice, if not in theory, much of the Prussian upper class accepted the economic and career benefits which the Empire could offer. At the other extreme of society, the working classes remained hostile to the Empire. Bismarck had attempted to neutralise the working class as a political force, on the one hand suppressing the Social Democratic Party and on the other, attempting to quell their discontent with a lavish programme of social security far in advance of the rest of Europe. To a certain extent, this application of stick and carrot was successful.

Yet after Bismarck's fall from power, when his suppressive legislation was not renewed, the spectre of workers' revolution evaporated. The Social Democrats quickly acquired a strong voice in politics (in the election of 1912 they became the largest single party in the Reichstag) and even became a stabilising force. They were a disciplined and coherent group; as one of their leader Gustav Noske rightly claimed during a Reichstag debate in 1907, "Where in Germany, except for the army, is there a greater measure of discipline than in the German Social Democratic Party and the modern trade unions?" But though they opposed the government on many issues, they were not really disenchanted with the nature of German society. More and more working men were becoming prosperous, and eventually moving up into the lower middle class. The number of Germans earning between 900 and 3000 Marks per annum had remained roughly static between 1862 and 1882. From 1882 to 1892 it grew steadily, and then in the next decade, suddenly tripled. Many other indicators, such as meat and coffee consumption, tell the same story. Thus, even those elements which were in theory opposed to the Empire, were directly or indirectly its beneficiaries.

A FLEET AGAINST ENGLAND

The fear that Imperial Germany might fragment into a multitude of conflicting interests, and thereby fall prey to her enemies, was a real one for the leaders of German society. Baron Friedrich von Holstein, for many years the *éminence grise* behind German diplomacy, wrote as late as 1907 that, "In the right psychological circumstances, the centrifugal forces will prove the stronger even in today's Germany... which is not a bloc but a mosaic of tribes." Many remedies were proposed. The prophet of the Right, Julius Langbehn, demanded a spiritual regeneration of the German people and the birth of a new idealism, for without it, disaster was imminent: "It has gradually become an open secret that the contemporary spiritual life of the German people is in a state of slow decay; according to some, even a rapid decay." These, the first words of his immensely successful book *Rembrandt als Erzieher*, galvanised German society into a search for new goals. Some young Germans found their inspiration in contact with the primal forces of nature, and formed the hiking groups known as "Wandervogel" which tramped the countryside at weekends and on public holidays. Others sought another truth in the new art forms of the "Jugendstil" and symbolism. But the bulk of the middle classes, and more slowly the upper classes, began to see Germany's ideal in terms of a colonial empire, and a strong navy which would make it possible. It was a reaction at first carefully fostered, and then skilfully manipulated, by the most intelligent and far-seeing members of the Imperial administration. Predominant among these men was Grand Admiral Alfred Tirpitz, the creator of the German battle fleet which was designed to challenge Britain's mastery of the seas.

Navalism appealed to Wilhelm II, who began to bombard his admirals with designs for ever bigger and better battleships. He was an excellent amateur draughtsman but his grasp of practical essentials was slight. A leading naval designer, the Italian Admiral Brin, responded to one of his more extravagant designs with the words: "The ship which your Majesty has designed will be the mightiest, the most terrible, and also the loveliest battleship ever seen. She would surpass anything now afloat, her masts would be the tallest in the world, the guns would outrange all others... This wonderful vessel has only one fault; if she were put on the water, she would sink like a lump of lead." The Emperor took the joke in good part, but continued to be a passionate supporter of the naval race. The deeper and more theoretical motives which lay behind the programme probably largely escaped his notice, but with his active support, the continued outward expansion gained a new strength. The many geographical and colonial societies, foremost among them the "Deutsche Kolonial Gesellschaft", the many academics who taught the necessity and ethical rightness of Germany's world role, and the manufacturers who saw new markets and new sources of supply in the colonies, all came together in support of an empire overseas. A Naval League was founded in 1898, and by 1908 had a million members throughout Germany; in 1896 the Emperor declared, "The German Empire has become a World Empire." He was a little premature, but by 1914, Germany possessed over a million square miles of territory overseas. She had achieved her "place in the sun".

This book comes to an end in 1914, just before Europe was plunged into the horror of the First World War. Germany's role in the outbreak of that war is as bitterly argued today as it has ever been. Whether Germany was responsible for pushing her enemies into a declaration of war, or whether she merely responded defensively to their attacks will probably never be resolved. But certainly her ambitious imperialism and bellicose utterances stimulated the atmosphere of extreme tension which existed in Europe for some years before war broke out. In 1918, the old order vanished almost overnight. The Hohenzollerns, the Wittelsbachs, and the other ruling families were forced to abdicate, and a republic emerged in their place. Now, after another war, even the fabric of the Empire has vanished—Dresden destroyed by bombing, Berlin by shellfire and systematic pillage, and scores of smaller cities changed out of recognition. As a result these photographs provide a visual record, perhaps unique, of the vanished world of Imperial Germany.

J. M. WHEATCROFT

THE ROMANTIC AGE

THE BLUE FLOWER

In September 1814 the rulers of Europe gathered in Vienna to remake the map of Europe after the Napoleonic Wars. As they did so, they took little account of the new emotional and social forces which the French Revolution had unleashed, and nowhere more so than in Germany. The humiliation of Germany at the hands of the French had fused together two strands in the national character: the spirit of the age of Romanticism, and the new-found patriotism of the youth of Germany. The romantic movement had taken a strong hold in Germany, but with a curiously historical bent. Friedrich von Hardenberg, who took the pen name of "Novalis" had written of the "blue flower", a symbol of the frail evanescent lyricism of the German past, of the great deeds of the Mediaeval Empire and the age of chivalry. Others took up the same theme, seeing in the German past the model of the future, a new idealism based on the power which a united Germany had once wielded. Perhaps the best example of this "Romantic patriot" is Ernst Moritz Arndt, who lived through the disasters under the French domination and the Revolution of 1848. He wrote of a new Germany, united into one nation, whose frontiers must extend

> So far as the German tongue be heard
> And God in heaven sings . . .

The rulers of the restored German states neither understood the new spirit of the age nor wished to do so. Under the careful guidance of the Austrian Chancellor, Metternich, all signs of radicalism and romanticism were carefully suppressed. But writers and artists kept alive the

theme of the new ideal of *Germany* and it gained strength despite the opposition of the authorities. Thus although Germany seemed tranquil on the surface in the period before the revolution of March 1848, all the seeds of discontent and rebellion were present. The new idealism was restricted almost exclusively to the educated middle class, and especially the young. In many of the smaller towns of Germany, the new spirit of the age was unknown: there and in the country, the concerns were with the economic problems of poor harvests and starvation. But even here the sense grew that the old order must change, and that better days must come. From these disparate forces, almost by accident, the many revolutions of 1848 were born.

The Elector's palace at Coblenz, probably the best example of French classical architecture in Germany: the view down Schlossstrasse

Above: Portrait of a Hamburg gentleman · Daguerreotype, pre-1846

Right: The daughter of the well-known Nuremberg bookseller, Johann Philipp Palm, executed for "sedition" by Napoleon in 1806 · Daguerreotype, 1840

The Royal train of King Maximilian II of Bavaria (1848–64), about 1856 · Photo: Maurer

Countess Charlotte von Fugger-Glött, at Munich, about 1860 · Photo: Hanfstaengl

The Besenbinder House in Hamburg, 1868

The colleagues of the famous chemist, Justus von Liebig, in their laboratory at Giessen ·
From left to right: Fresenius, Will, Bullock, Gardener and Hoffman · Daguerreotype, about 1840

The chemist's shop in Langenbiehlau, Lower Silesia (today Bielawa in Poland) ·
Daguerreotype, about 1846 (Dost Collection, Berlin)

A dancer, in a coloured stereoscopic daguerreotype of a type very popular during the 1850s

An art study, *Nude in the mirror* · Many copies of this picture were in circulation about 1850 · Daguerreotype

Sophie Leonore Schleiden (died 1856) · She was the wife of Dr. Andreas Schleiden, one of the governing council of the
free city of Hamburg · Daguerreotype · Stelzner

On the left, Frau von Braunschweig, on the right, Caroline Stelzner, wife of the photographer C. F. Stelzner ·
Daguerreotype · Stelzner

Above: The Yellow Drawing Room of the house at 44 Gartenstrasse, Stuttgart, looking through into the Blue Room · The house was built in 1860 by Morlock for Kommerzienrat Carl Jobst

Right: The well-known writer Eduard Mörike and his family on a visit in July 1865 to a relative, Dr. Carl Abraham Mörike, a pharmacist at Neuenstadt on Kocher ·
From left to right: the pharmacist and his wife, Eduard's wife Klara, the pharmacist's niece, Marie von Schott · In the foreground, Eduard's eldest daughter Fanny · The writer poses reading ·
Coloured stereoscopic daguerreotype

A boating picnic, about 1860

A group aboard a steamer, about 1860

On September 27, 1857, the new Grosshesseloh Bridge over the Isar, near Munich, was tested for stress. The heaviest engine of the day, *München*, crossed the bridge pulling waggons loaded with 105 tons of peat

The Maxburg in Munich
about 1856, looking from
Lenbachplatz. On the
left, the start of the street
which housed the
state pawn office ·
Photo: Hanfstaengl

The Round Tower and
part of the fortifications
of the town wall of
Munich near the old
produce market,
about 1856

The erection of the statue *Bavaria* at Munich · *Above:* Transporting the head from the workshops of Ferdinand von Miller in the Theresienwiese · *Left:* positioning the torso · Talbotype · Löcherer, 1850

Prince Adalbert of Bavaria (1828–1875) photographed about 1866 · He was an uncle of the ill-fated Ludwig II ·
Photo: Hanfstaengl

Count Carl von Butler, Lord Chamberlain to the King of Bavaria, and a Major-General in the Bavarian army, portrayed in hunting costume, about 1865 · Photo: Hanfstaengl

Above: Baroness Frederike von Gumppenberg, a lady in waiting at the Court of Bavaria in the mid-1860s · Photo: Löcherer

Right: View from Rosenheimerstrasse towards the centre of Munich, about 1858 · Photo: Böttger

Above: The main railway station at Munich, looking back down the tracks in the direction of the
city centre · In the background is the station hall, built by Friedrich Bürklein between 1847 and 1849

Right: The main departure platform at Munich East railway station, about 1858 · Photo: Böttger

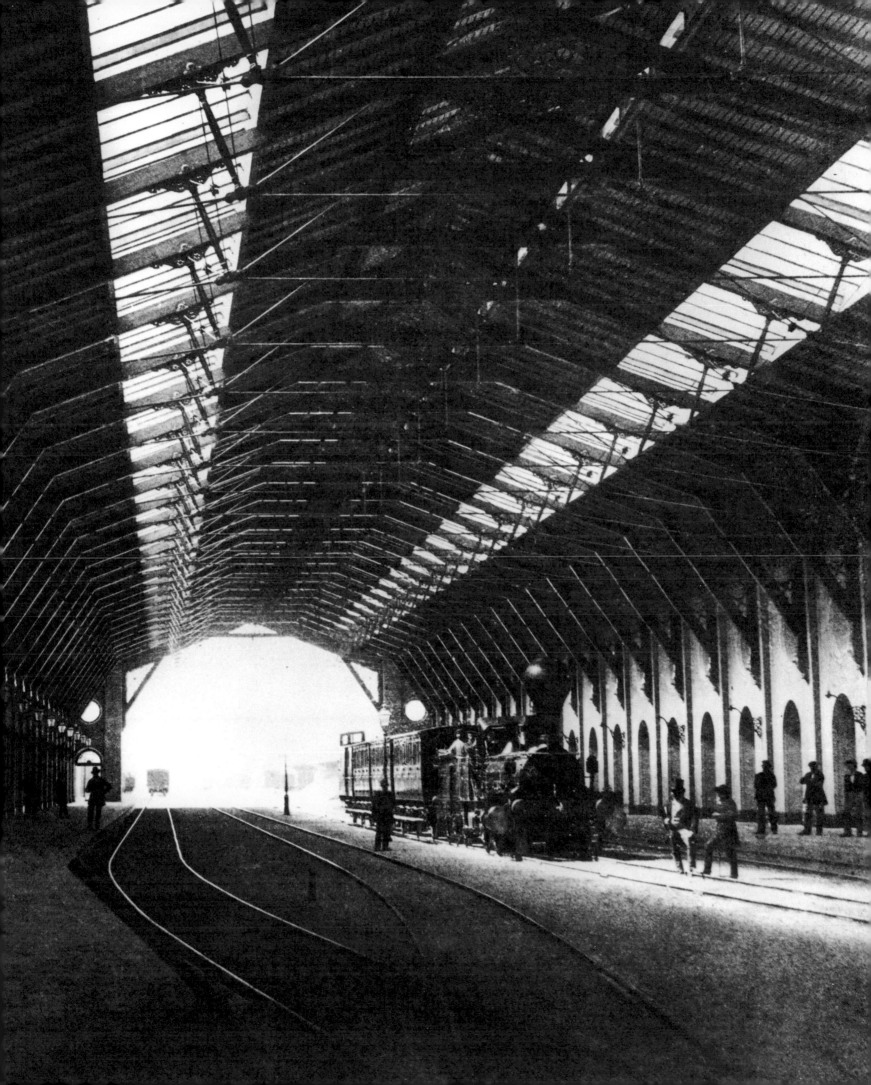

Franz Hanfstaengl, the photographer and founder of the well-known fine art publisher · self portrait, about 1860

Kaspar von Steinsdorf, the Mayor
of Munich ·
Photo: Hanfstaengl

Baron Adolf von Gumppenberg and
his wife Karoline, photographed
about 1860 · Photo: Hanfstaengl

The Church of Our Lady, Munich,
seen from the tower of St. Peter's
Church. A section of a panorama
produced by G. Göttger on the occasion
of Munich's 700th
anniversary celebrations in 1858

Above: The Isar Gate at Munich, about 1856

Overleaf: The 500th engine to leave the Maffei factory in the Hirschau near Munich in 1864 · The photograph was presented to the owner of the factory (standing in the foreground) by his workers "with respect and gratitude" · The firm still exists today · Photo: Albert

Above: View of Schloss Hohenschwangau, near the village of Füssen. From the collection of the Duke of Saxe-Altenburg

Below: A bedroom in the Schloss with walls decorated with scenes drawn from German legends · In this castle, Ludwig II spent part of his childhood and youth, and was inspired by the world of German myth

Right: King Ludwig II of Bavaria, during his brief engagement to Sophie (left) the sister of the Empress Elisabeth of Austria · He succeeded to the throne in 1864, and in twenty-two years nearly beggared his country with his grandiose mania for building fairy-tale castles · He was the most noted of Wagner's patrons · In June 1886 he was declared insane and deposed, and within of three days was found drowned in the Starnberger See, with his "keeper", Dr. Gudden · The strain of madness was strong in the Wittelsbach family: his brother Otto also went mad · Photo: Albert, 1867

Left: Countess Caroline von Butler, a lady in waiting at the Court of Bavaria, in the early 1860s · Photo: Hohbach

Above: The Villa Texas in Stuttgart, which was built about 1860 for the former Texan consul to the Kingdom of Württemberg, Joseph Sauter and his rich father · At that time the building was still surrounded by vineyards · Texas remained an independent state until 1845, when it was incorporated into the United States of America · Photo: Brandseph

The first horse-drawn bus service
in Stuttgart, 1869

Above: Stuttgart market place, about 1870

Right: Two women from the family of a prominent local physician,
Dr. Schlossberger, at Feuerbach, near Stuttgart

Left: The passionate nationalist and writer of patriotic songs, Ernst Moritz Arndt (1769–1860) · He was elected to represent the fifteenth electoral district in the Prussian Rhineland at the National Assembly in Frankfurt in 1848 · This photograph was published in Frankfurt in 1848 · Daguerreotype · Seib

Right: A corner of the historic Römerberg area of Frankfurt · All the great ceremonies of the old Holy Roman Empire were enacted here · The picture shows the Salt House on the corner of Wedelgasse · In the background is the tower of St. Paul's Church in which the meetings of the National Assembly were held in 1848–9 · This photograph was taken prior to the alterations of 1861 · Photo: Mylius

Overleaf: The banks of the River Main at Frankfurt about 1860 · On the right, the cathedral before it was damaged by fire

The revolutionaries of 1848
Johannes Detmold, a right-wing delegate
to the National Assembly of 1848 ·
Daguerreotype · Seib

C. Fuchs, a delegate to the National
Assembly, 1848 · Daguerreotype · Biow

Left: The Römerberg area, with the Limpurg house on the left. On the right is the building known as the Römer, where the coronation of the Holy Roman Emperors was celebrated. In July and August 1848 the artisans met in this hall while the middle classes debated the future of the nation in St. Paul's Church nearby · Photo: Mylius, 1864

Above: The Römerberg with the Schiller monument in the foreground · This statue, by Dielmann, was unveiled on November 10, 1859, in commemoration of the hundredth anniversary of the poet's birth · Photo: Mylius

Skating on a fishpond in Frankfurt about 1860

The Mall in Frankfurt about 1869

Near right: The castle church and old tax office at Marburg on Lahn about 1850 · Daguerreotype

Below: The pioneering agricultural chemist, Justus von Liebig (1803–73) and his family, about 1844 · Daguerreotype

Far right: The port at Coblenz, where the Moselle joins the Rhine

Right: For decades, there was no railway bridge over the Rhine and travellers had to cross on foot by the pontoon bridge at Oberkassel before continuing to Aachen · The porters formed a guild which lasted until the beginning of the twentieth century · This photograph shows the Düsseldorf porters' guild, about 1860

Below: The ferryboat *Loreley I* built in Holland in 1866, on the Rhine opposite St. Goarshausen

The building of Cologne Cathedral had
been stopped during the middle
ages · It was recommenced in 1842 · The
photograph shows the cathedral from
the south, about 1858–59

St. Gereon's gate, forming part of the mediaeval fortifications of the city of Cologne

Cologne: the haymarket, with the house where the famous architect Jacob Ignaz Hittorf (1792–1867) was born

Top left: Karl Marx, born in
Trier in 1818, died in London
in 1883

Bottom left: Friedrich Engels,
born in Barmen in 1820,
died in London in 1892 · The
two first met in Cologne in 1842

St. Anthony's foundry, one of the oldest in the Ruhr (founded 1758) · It was a
precursor of the Gute-Hoffnungs-Hütte (see the section "Made in Germany") ·
Photo: Gunther, 1864

The shipyard of "Jacobi, Haniel and Hüyssen", a leading
ironworks in Duisburg-Rührort · Ships were built here
during the period 1829–1899 · Photo: Gunther, 1864

In 1842 Hamburg was devastated by a fire which lasted four days, destroying a huge area of the city · "By the still light of day, you could see... the corpse of the city" (Friedrich Hebbel, 1846)

Right: The Adolphplatz in Hamburg, looking towards the Stock Exchange, the Grossen Burstah and the tower of St. Catherine's Church, at the time of the rebuilding after the fire · Daguerreotype (image reversed) · Stelzner, 1847

Below: The ruins of the Alster district – the Jungfernstieg and the Lombard Bridge after the fire of 1842 Daguerreotype · Stelzner

The ruins of St. Nicholas' Church, Hamburg, after the fire of 1842 · Daguerreotype · Stelzner

Top left: Two Hamburg students – Wilhelm Andres and Edmund Johann Kruss · The student societies (Burschenschaften) were thought to be hotbeds of revolution and were suppressed in many German states · Daguerreotype, 1842

Top right: A lawyer, Dr. Heinrich Nicholas von Beseler, in the uniform of a 1st lieutenant of cavalry in the Hamburg militia · Daguerreotype · Biow

Left: The critic and sati Moritz Gottlieb Sap (1795–1858) · From 1 he edited a comic pa called *The Humour* Daguerreotype · Stelz 1

Right: The Mayo Hamb Ascan W. Lutteroth (17 1867), with his Charlotte, about 1

Above: The miniaturist Caroline Stelzner (1808–1875), portrayed by her husband
C. F. Stelzner, in 1843

Right: A Hamburg merchant, Daniel Runge and his wife, about 1844 · His brother was the
painter Philipp Otto Runge · Daguerreotype

Left and above: Hamburg shipyard · Talbotype · Fuchs, about 1850

Overleaf left: Old Mother Albers, who sold vegetables to the Stelzner family, about 1845 · Daguerreotype · Stelzner

Overleaf right: Street in the port of Hamburg · Photo: Höge, 1864

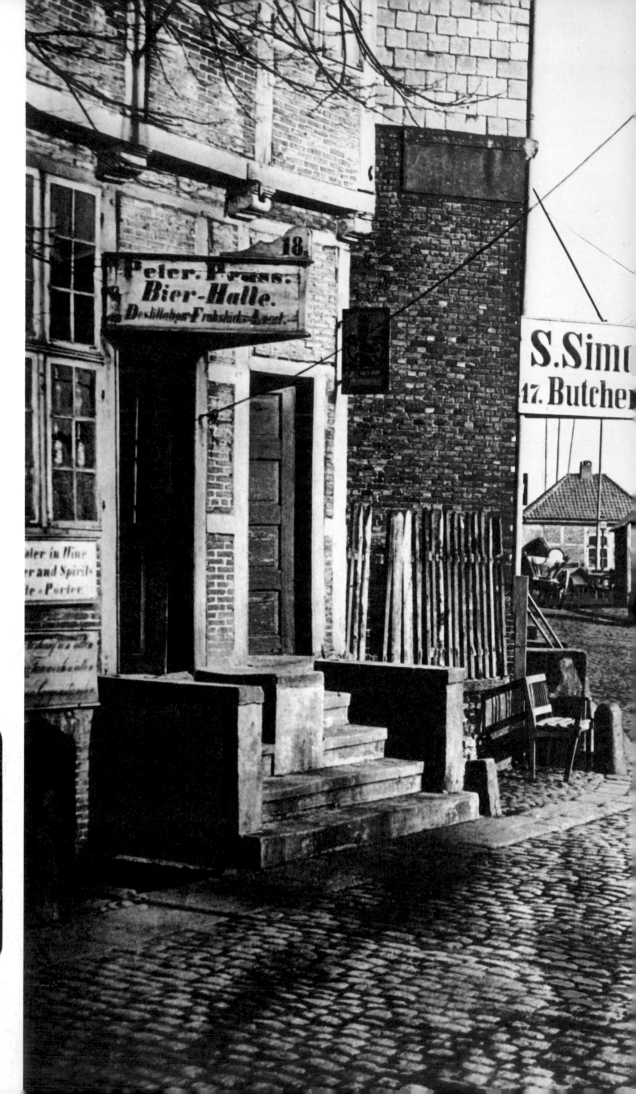

Country people from the Vierlande, the lowlands which lay surrounded by dykes between the rivers Elbe and Bille, seen here at Hamburg market about 1860

A new crane on the dockside at Hamburg about 1858

Hamburg Customs House in the port · Photographer Biow set
up his studio in its tower in 1842 · Photo: Fuchs, 1856

A prosperous Hamburg merchant, Johann Philipp Ludwig Bartels with his family ·
Daguerreotype · Stelzner, 1847

The lower port at Hamburg, seen from the "Kehrwiede", 1868 · Hamburg was the largest port in Germany
and the third largest city in 1870, after Berlin and Munich · The famous Hamburg America line was established in 1847,
a continuation of the port's long Hanseatic trading tradition

Left: The Jungfernbrücke (Maiden Bridge) in Berlin, about 1845 · Daguerreotype

Below: The Waisenbrücke (Orphan Bridge) in Berlin, about 1842 · Daguerreotype · Sachse

Right: The brothers Jakob and Wilhelm Grimm, who were pioneers in the field of folklore (the famous *Fairytales* are a familiar example) · There was much in their work which could be used to show the historical and legendary foundations of a unified Germany · This picture shows them around 1842 · Daguerreotype · Biow

The palace precincts and bridge in Berlin,
about 1847 · The main body of the
palace can be seen in the top right-hand
corner · The bridge was demolished
in 1892 · Daguerreotype

Juggglers in Berlin, about 1846

1

Ernst Jakob Renz, the famous circus owner · His highly trained equestrian teams found much favour with the Empress Elisabeth of Austria: seen here in Berlin

The Brandenburg
Gate in Berlin,
about 1868

3

Page 112: Countess Edith Hacke, born 1821, a lady-in-waiting to Queen Elisabeth of Prussia, wife of Friedrich Wilhelm IV, Berlin, 1856

Page 113: Princess Radziwill : She belonged to the small inner circle of the court of Friedrich Wilhelm IV

Left: The statue of the Great Elector which stood on the Long Bridge in Berlin, about 1860 · The statue was the work of Andreas Schlüter · Photo: Krone

Above: Friedrich Wilhelm IV, King of Prussia, 1840–1861 · He refused the Imperial throne offered him by the National Assembly at Frankfurt saying it was "A dog collar, with which they will chain me to the Revolution of 1848" · Daguerreotype · Biow, 1847

Berlin, "Athens on the Spree" – so called because of its
imposing classical buildings · The Gendarmenmarkt,
with the German cathedral, the Royal theatre, and the
French cathedral are shown here, about 1866

Below: Soldiers playing cards, about 1860

Right: Christmas at the house of the Jamrath family, Berlin 1863 ·
The traditional table on which presents were piled is decorated with
evergreens and candles

19

Above: Alexander von Humboldt (1769–1859), the
famous explorer · Daguerreotype · Biow, 1847

Below: The painter Peter von Cornelius (1783–1867)

1   The sculptor Christian Daniel Rauch (1777–1857) · Daguerreotype · Biow, 1847

Above: The Waisenbrücke (Orphan Bridge) in Berlin, about 1855 · Photo: Ahrendts

Left: Emil Devrient, a popular actor at the court theatre in Berlin, about 1845 · Daguerreotype

Right: The weekly market in the Alexanderplatz, Berlin, about 1863

3

Above: The Russian ambassador to Berlin, Baron von Budberg, and his family, about 1860

Right: The dome of the palace and the palace bridge in Berlin, about 1860 · Photo: Krone

Above: The house of Niels Jens Brodersen at Westerland, in the Sylt peninsula ·
This was part of Denmark until 1864 · Melainotype, 1862

Right: A summer meeting of an artists' club, in an open air cafe at the
Caffamacherreihe in Hamburg · Such meetings often had political overtones ·
Daguerreotype · Stelzner, 1843

The small single-track railway station in front of the Holsten Gate in Lübeck · In the centre foreground,
a statue of Mercury on the Puppenbrücke (Doll's Bridge), carrying a parcel!

Above: Houses on the Bauernmarkt (now the Koberg), Lübeck, about 1855

Overleaf: View from the ramparts (later demolished), Lübeck, about 1869

Left: A servant girl of Lübeck, about 1860

Right: The town gate of Lübeck before 1850 · After 1850
a second entrance was cut so that pedestrians did not have
to wait while carts passed through · Daguerreotype

Facing page: Top left: A fisherman from the village of Schlutup, in summer dress

Bottom left: The same, in winter dress

Top right: A fisherwoman from Gothmund, about 1860

Bottom right: Master locksmith Strohkark as a sapper in the Lübeck town militia, about 1860

Above: Fisherwomen from Travemünde, near Hamburg, taking live fish to market, about 1860

Overleaf: Carl Hermann Dittmer (1793–1865), a senator of Lübeck, about 1855

35

Previous page: The Breite Strasse (Broad Street) in Lübeck · In the background, the Jacobi tower · 1860

Below: Laying the foundations for a railway bridge at Bremen, in 1865

Bremen market place, in 1865 · In the centre of the picture stands the Roland Column,
which was a symbol of the charter held by the market

9

Bremen personalities
From top left to bottom right: Rudolf Rönneberg as a Böse Jaeger, 1865
Fire chief Theodor Hoffmann, Bremen, 1867
Corporal Mayer, Bremen, 1866
"Martin Weber, formerly pastry cook of this good city, and now a man of private means" · Bremen, 1862
Von Helferich, the bandmaster of Bremen's military band · Bremen, 1852
Friedrich Luley, a hunter · Bremen, about 1870

Bremen: the Roland
Column, and the old
Stock Exchange on the
right of the picture,
1863

Above: Steamship departure point at Kalkstrasse, Bremen, 1864

Right: Ship's captain Geerken at Bremen, 1858 · The famous North German Lloyd
Shipping Line was founded at Bremen in 1856

1

Above: The painter Leo Gey from Hanover · He specialised in historical subjects and was a pupil of
Julius Schnorr von Carolsfeld · His work included frescoes in the Marienburg, in Meissen and Osnabrück
On the photograph, the dedication reads: "Remember the original of this in friendship over the years
Your loving and devoted Leo Gey · Hanover 1860"

Right: The house of Peter Bernhard Heyn, Schmiedstrasse, Hanover, in 1857

Left: C. Fehn, who became the head riding master at the court of King George V of Hanover

Right: The first market day in the new town market at Hanover, 1863 · Photo: Liebsch

Left: The town council of Cassel · The lord mayor sits in the front row, fourth from the left · Daguerreotype, 1850

Above: An open air concert in front of the Aue Gate in Cassel, about 1860

Below: The market place at Leipzig about 1865 · On the left the old office of weights and measures, in the middle the Koch House

Right: The old town hall in Leipzig about 1857

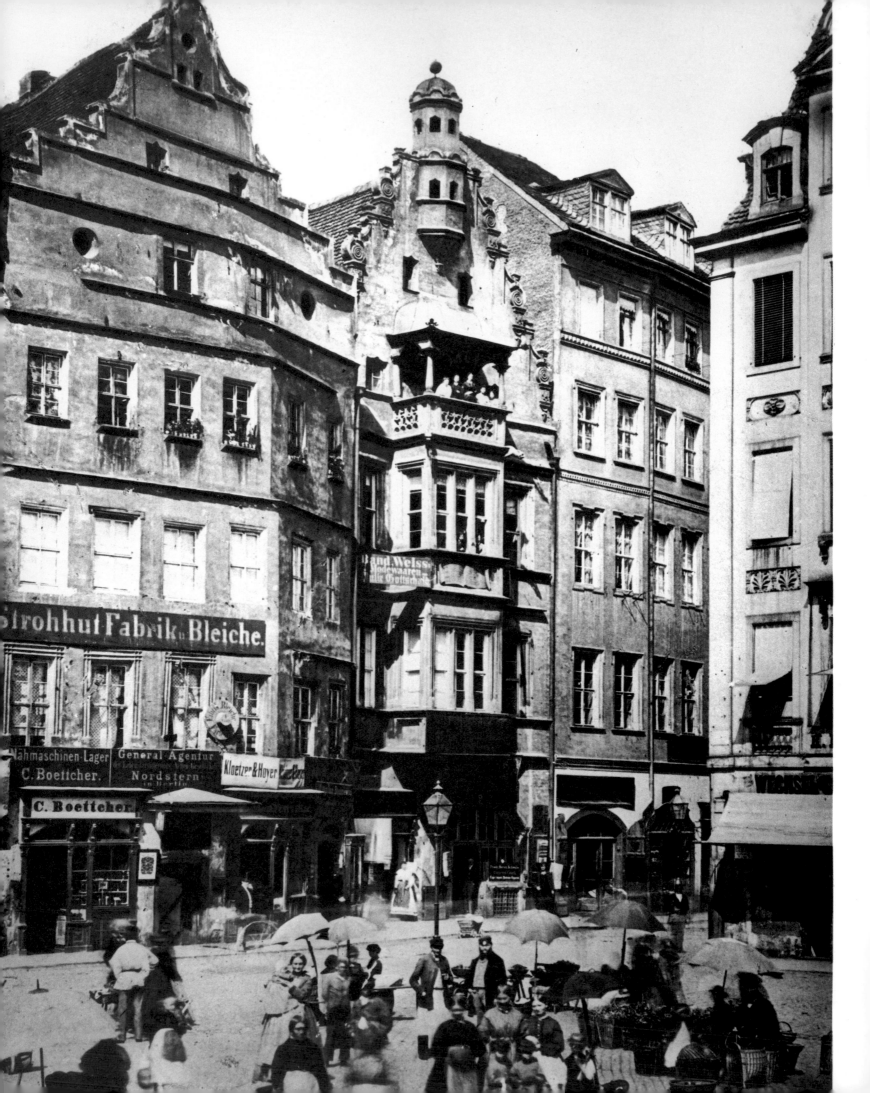

Left: The Bartel House on the market place at Leipzig, about 1868

Above: The centre of the German book trade in the Nikolaifriedhof in Leipzig, about 1860

The Augustus Bridge, the Court Church and the
Royal Palace at Dresden · On the right of the picture
above the river bank, stands the "Italian Village",
and behind it the famous picture gallery built by
Gottfried Semper · Photo: Krone, 1860–1865

The bearded Crown Prince of Saxony, Albert, playing skittles at Dresden in the early 1860s · He was the closest friend of the Emperor Franz Joseph of Austria, who was also his cousin · He fought on the Austrian side in the war of 1866 with Prussia, and distinguished himself in the war of 1870 against France · He came to the throne in 1873 and reigned until his death in 1902 · Photo: Krone

The Dresden theatre after the
disastrous fire of 1869 · Photo: Krone
The painter and graphic artist Ludwig Richter
(1803–1884) · He was *the* illustrator of the
German Romantic movement · From 1835,
he was professor at the Academy in his home
town of Dresden, which rapidly became
famous as a centre for wood engraving
Photo: Krone

The painter and grafic artist Ludwig Richter (1803–1884): He was *the* illustrator of the German Romantic movement · From 1835, he was professor at the academy in his home town of Dresden, which rapidly became famous as a centre for woodingraving · Photo: Krone

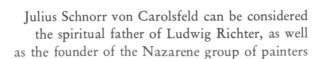

Julius Schnorr von Carolsfeld can be considered the spiritual father of Ludwig Richter, as well as the founder of the Nazarene group of painters

The Kotzch house with its vineyards in Dresden-Loschwitz. Ludwig Richter
worked here in the summer months of 1852 and 1857 · During his second stay
here, the illustrations were produced for Schiller's "Lied von der Glocke"

Above: The bank of the River Elbe at Dresden, with the Royal Church and the
Brühl terrace in the centre of the picture, and the Opera House behind ·
In the foreground is the steamer *Dresden,* built in 1838 · Photo: Krone

Left: Portrait of a lady, Dresden, about 1850 · Photo: Krone

The first festival of the German Choral Association, held at Dresden. The photograph shows the dedication of the association's banner · Cultural gatherings like this became pressure groups for a united Germany

The Brühl Terrace in Dresden with statues representing the Four Seasons ·
Photo: Krone, 1860–5

Self portrait of the photographer Hermann Krone surrounded by his apparatus, Dresden, 1865

The gendarmes and military band of the grand ducal court in Weimar, about 1850

A group of photographs by Hermann Krone taken between 1860 and 1865

Above left: The market place and St. Elisabeth's Church in Breslau
Above right: The market place in Görlitz
Below left: The banks of the River Neisse at Görlitz, which now forms the border between East Germany and Poland
Below right: View across the rooftops of Görlitz

1   The market place in Breslau · Photo: Krone, 1860–5

Left: The Jopengasse, the most attractive street in old Danzig, with St. Mary's Church behind it, about 1865

Above: View of Danzig, about 1865

The fine Renaissance building
which housed the Danzig
Town armoury, about 1865

Danzig market place, with the tower known locally as "Kiek in de Kok" behind, about 1865

1

The Artus, or Junkerhof, which housed the Danzig stock exchange, in the Langen Markt (Long Market) about 1865

Overleaf: The High Gate of Danzig, about 1865

THE
SECOND
EMPIRE

BLOOD AND IRON

The Empire was created as Bismarck had proclaimed it would be, not through "speeches and shooting matches and songs" but through "blood and iron". The defeat of Austria on the field of Königgrätz marked the first stage, the destruction of the Armies of France the second stage. The final act came on January 18, 1871, in the great Hall of Mirrors in the Palace of Versailles, which spelt out to the world how high Germany had risen and how low France had fallen since the great days of Louis XIV. The scene was soon enshrined in myth, and recorded, inaccurately, in the famous painting by Anton von Werner; the words of an eye-witness, however, convey the emotion of the occasion. The Crown Prince of Prussia had fought brilliantly in the wars which established the empire; now he stood at his father's side as the Crown of Germany was offered.

"After the Te Deum had been sung, the King, followed by us all, betook himself to the platform, that had been built in front of the Salon de la Guerre, and upon which the junior officers were already stationed with the flags and standards. He summoned the standard-bearers, with the war-torn flags of the first battalion of the First Regiment, Regiment of Foot-guards and the three from his Grenadier Regiment, one of whom also bore a flag that had been shot to pieces, so that they came straight to him and stood directly behind him, side by side with me. To the right and left of this middle group—surely an unusual one—the German reigning Princes and Hereditary Princes took their place and behind them flags and standards came to rest.

After his Majesty had read a short address to the German Sovereigns in his usual rough tones, Count Bismarck stepped forward. He looked quite furiously out of humour as he read the address 'to the German nation'. He read tonelessly, using an official manner and without

any trace of festive mood. At the words 'Extender of the Reich' I noticed a convulsive movement through the whole assembly, which otherwise remained without a sound.

Now the Grand Duke of Baden, with the natural, quiet dignity that was so characteristic of him, stepped forward and cried aloud with his right hand raised: 'Long live His Imperial Majesty, the Emperor Wilhelm!' A thundering cheer, repeated at least six times, thrilled through the room, while the flags and standards waved over the head of the new Emperor of Germany and 'Hail Thou in the Victor's Crown' resounded. This moment was powerfully striking, indeed overpowering so, and made a wonderful sight. I bent my knee before the Emperor and kissed his hand; he raised me up and embraced me with deep emotion. I cannot describe my feelings but everybody understood. I even saw unmistakable emotion among the standard-bearers.

Now the Princes, one after the other, offered their congratulations, which the Emperor received with a friendly shake of the hand, whereupon a file past took place, but on account of the unavoidable press of people it lacked any proper formality. The Emperor next walked along the line of flags and their bearers, stepped from the platform towards those standing in the front, and as he walked through the hall, addressed a few words in passing to the officers and men standing on both sides. I had commanded the band to play the Hohenfriedberg March as soon as the Emperor prepared to leave the hall, so that His Majesty left the assembly to these magnificent sounds, and so, greeted by the cheers of the Headquarters Guard, he left the palace."

Outside, representatives of the army stood waiting for the news and to cheer their new Emperor. The German Empire had been reborn.

Page 183:
The coronation of Wilhelm, Prince of Prussia, in Königsberg, on October 18, 1861 · An uncompromising reactionary, he had fled to England to escape the revolution of 1848 · He served for years as Regent, through his brother's incapacity to rule · Although he became German Emperor in 1871, he always considered himself as "King of Prussia", avoiding the use of the Imperial title · Königsberg now lies in Russia

Left: The formal photograph taken at the close of the Congress of German Princes, on September 1, 1863 at Frankfurt on Main. This crucial meeting, which the Prussian King avoided, accepted the reforming plans of the Emperor Franz Joseph of Austria (in the centre, on the steps). But without Prussian agreement it was an empty gesture: three years later Prussia excluded Austria from Germany · Among those attending were King Johann of Saxony, translator of Dante and author in his own right (the small white-haired figure, eighth from the left), and the blind King of Hanover, said to have been blinded as a child while twirling a dog chain; his arm is linked with his attendant's (right) ·
Photo: Albert

The battle at the Düppel redoubt during the German-Danish war of 1864 · The German Confederation, represented by Prussia and Austria, went to war with Denmark over the disputed duchies of Schleswig and Holstein · This was the first European war to demonstrate the terrible effectiveness of modern weapons, shown here by the destruction of the sixth bastion

The German
corvette *Arcona*
during the
German-Danish
war

Above: The palisades of the Düppel redoubt

Top right: The fourth bastion and its blockhouse surrounded by twelve-pounder smoothbore cannon · The shattered blockhouse, believed by the Danes to be proof against artillery fire, shows the efficiency of the rifled Prussian guns

Bottom right: A battery of Austrian heavy artillery, directed against the Danish defences at Fünen

Above: The architect of victory against Austria in 1866 and France in 1871: the Chief of the Prussian General Staff, Helmuth von Moltke (1800–1891) · He is seen here working in his study in the General Staff building on the Königsplatz in Berlin, known colloquially as the "Grossen Bude" (The rabbit warren)

Right: The Austro-Prussian war of 1866 · The entry of the victorious army into Berlin and the service of thanksgiving by the statue of Berolina, on September 21, 1866

The homecoming of the troops to Berlin and their reception
at the Brandenburg Gate on September 20, 1866
Photo: Jamrath

Above: The damage to the Paris suburb of
St. Cloud during the siege of the city in the
Franco-Prussian war of 1870–71
Right: Stocks of cannon balls in the fortress of
Metz in the war of 1870–71

1

Captured artillery in Northern France, 1870–71

A prisoner of war camp at Coblenz during the Franco-Prussian war · Photo: Kilger

A volunteer medical team, 1870–71

1   Staff officers in quarters at St. Brice-Darc, 1870

Otto von Bismarck enjoyed a close relationship with the well-known
singer, Pauline Lucca (1841–1908) · She first came to Berlin in 1861 ·
Bismarck was renowned in his youth for his many affairs

The drawing room of the Hotel Schwan at Frankfurt on Main, where
on May 10, 1871 Bismarck and Jules Favre signed the peace treaty
which ended the Franco-Prussian war; the terms were harsh, but the
French had no choice but to accept · Photo: Pohl

The first celebration of the victory at Sedan in front of the statue of
Frederick the Great on September 30, 1870; Sedan Day was
celebrated every year thereafter as a popular holiday

The entry of the Bavarian troops into Munich after their return from
the French campaign of 1871 · They passed from the Victory Gate
(in the background) down Ludwigstrasse to the Odeonplatz ·
Photo: Albert

05

Delegations from the
Prussian Guards
Landwehr division
(right) and the Second
Bavarian Corps
(below) at the Hall
of Mirrors in the Palace
of Versailles for the
proclamation of the
empire, on
January 18, 1871

Above: The reception in June 1871 for the returning troops in the Rossmarkt at Frankfurt on Main

Overleaf: Souvenir of the war of 1870–71 with the names of the battlefields

METZ
TOUL
PARIS
DREUX
MADELAINE
BELLÊMES

ORLÉANS
MEUNG
BEAUGENCY
FRÉTEVAL
DUNEAU
LE MANS

"MADE IN GERMANY"

The Empire had been won by blood and iron but its place in the world was ensured by the growing might of industry and commerce. The three words "Made in Germany" carried on all German goods (a result of the British Merchandise Marks Act, which required a label of origin) became the slogan of Germany's economic imperialism. In Russia and England, patriots mounted campaigns against the increasing dominance of German goods in every market, which they claimed was driving domestic industry into bankruptcy. The fear of Germany's military might which had followed from the war of 1870-71 was now matched by the new fear of the Empire's booming economy.

The Industrial Revolution had come comparatively late to a Germany still disunited. But if political unity had to wait until 1871, the country was already bound together by links of commerce. The first railway line was opened from Nuremberg to Fürth in 1835, to be followed rapidly by many more, providing cheap and rapid communications. New roads were built—by 1850, Germany possessed about 50,000 kilometres of modern, metalled roads—as well as canals which made full use of the extensive network of rivers as a means of transport. New industries sprang up to take advantage of the revolution in communications, and the Ruhr became a centre of many heavy industrial plants where only a few small companies had existed before. An important element in this rapid expansion was the Zollverein or Customs Union, established under Prussian leadership on January 1, 1836; other states set up similar unions in imitation of the Prussian model. By 1870 the internal barriers to trade within Germany had largely disappeared.

Under the Empire the full advantages of economic unification were achieved, although the great seaports of Hamburg and Bremen stayed outside the German Customs Union until 1888. German industry benefited from the earlier industrial revolution in Britain, and avoided the pitfalls already exposed. Germany invested in "new" industries like the electrical and chemical industries with impressive results: by 1913 half the international trade in electrical goods was in German hands, and by 1900, Germany produced 90% of the world's chemical dyes. New developments in technology enabled Germany to exploit the resources in iron ore of the newly-acquired province of Lorraine: by 1910 Germany was producing twice as much steel as Great Britain, an almost exact reversal of the position in 1870. Changes operated in every sector of German industry and commerce, one often complementing another. German banking grew into a powerful force moulding industrial companies into cartels and structures of increasing strength and efficiency. Foreign competitors marvelled at the lengths to which German salesmen would go to get an order, and the terms of credit they were able to offer. The German shipping industry, initially tiny compared with the British merchant fleet, grew steadily, largely by carrying German goods to the export markets. Germany radiated confidence and efficency to the world, and every new railway engine or child's toy marked "Made in Germany" was a further reminder of her seemingly limitless power to expand.

If the expansion had continued quite steadily, even during the lean years of the economic

depression, its real effects became felt within German society from the mid-1890s. New fortunes were easily made: the number of millionaires nearly tripled between 1892 and 1912. The workers and the middle classes enjoyed a steady improvement in the standard of living, especially in the cities where many of the tensions in German society had bred. New inventions and conveniences gave them objects on which to spend their money; a Sunday suit was no longer a fantasy to the working man, and holidays became a luxury enjoyed by many. Germans took to the motor car and the telephone with relish, and gained a reputation among their more staid European neighbours for being gadget-mad.

The idols of the new Germany were men of business like Fritz Krupp the "armaments king" (despite some unsavoury scandals attached to his name), Walter Rathenau, and the shipowner Albert Ballin. The most exclusive of the old aristocracy might sneer at them as "nouveaux riches" but the middle classes made them into heroes; even Wilhelm II professed to admire their services to Germany. Richard Dehmel wrote of Albert Ballin:

> It is he who brings order to the noisy masses
> He who earns the private thanks of people living in narrow streets,
> A captain who guides many ships…

The Captains of Industry became, with the traditional holders of power, the new controllers of the destiny of the nation. To the ethical and spiritual goals of a united Germany were added the new aims of a commercial Empire which stretched across the globe.

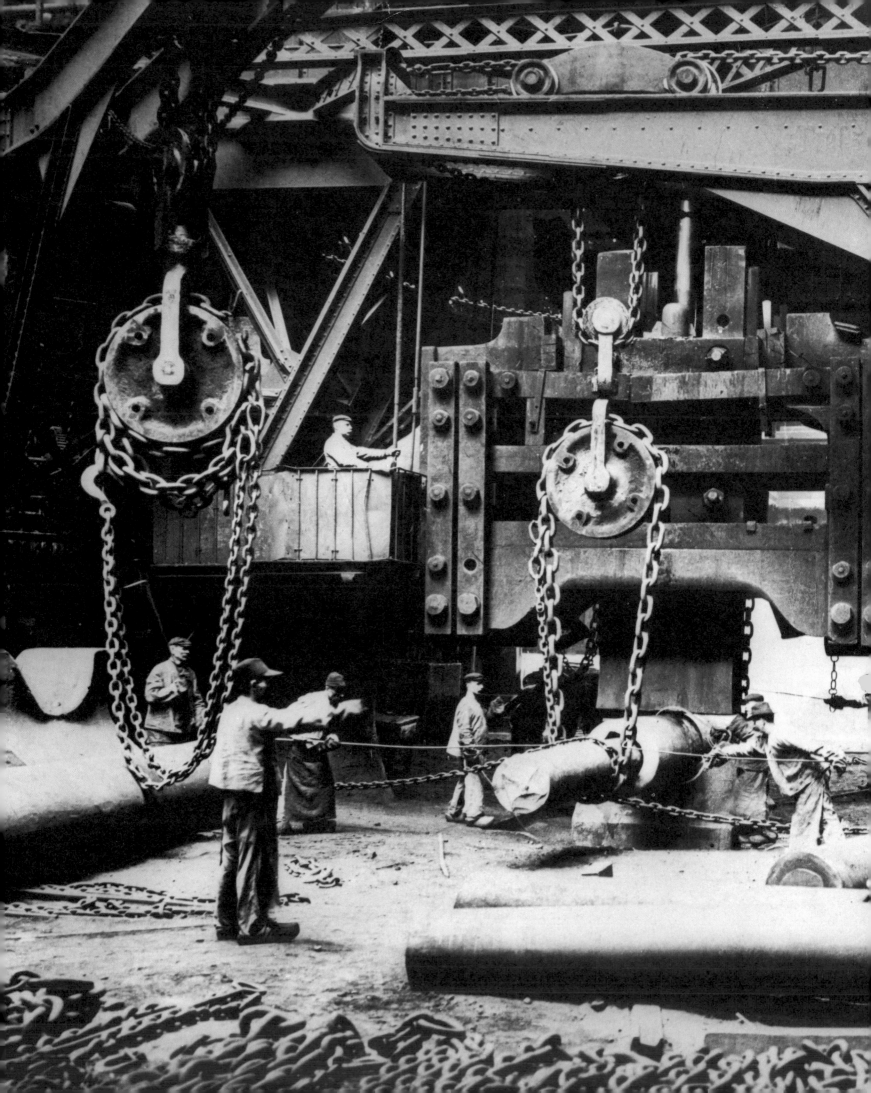

Page 211: An electric mail coach made by Vollmer and Kühlstein

Left: Fritz, the first steam-operated hammer installed in the Krupp plant at Essen, in 1861 · Alfred Krupp named it after his son

The Oberhausen steelworks of the "Gute Hoffnungs Hütte", about 1880

The Zeppelin "Viktoria Luise" at Munich on October 24, 1912 · The guests of honour
and army officers crowd around the airship's cabin after its landing on the Oberwiesenfeld ·
The notice reads NO SMOKING for obvious reasons · Photo: Schmitz

The first "Parseval" airship landing at Munich on October 14, 1909

Otto Lilienthal attempts powerless flight from the May Heights in Steglitz in the spring of 1893

21   Otto Lilienthal trys gliding from the Fliegerburg at Lichterfelde-Ost on August 16, 1894

A flying display at Frankfurt on Main, the occasion of the first German overland flight from Frankfurt to Mannheim in August 1910

Left: The victor, Jeannin, in his "Aviator" machine

Right: A pioneer airman Plochmann in his machine, flying over the start of the course

Overleaf: The steam-engine "Brugg" was built in 1856 by the heavy-engineering firm of Maffei at Munich

Previous spread: The platform hall of Lehrter Station in Berlin, 1872

Below: Steam omnibus made by the firm of Hermann Michaelis at Chemnitz in Saxony, about 1890

Right: The suspension railway at
Barmen-Elberfeld, 1905

Below: A steam tramcar of the South German
Railway Company of Darmstadt, seen in
Rheinstrasse, about 1900

The inventor of the Diesel engine, Rudolf Diesel and his family, at their house in Giselastrasse,
Munich · The two visitors are Professor Souvage and F. Dyckhoff

Above: The employees of the Benz factory in the early days of the motor car, 1894

Right: Carl and Clara Benz travelling in a Benz-Viktoriawagen, 1893 · He was one of the pioneers of motor car construction and the use of the internal combustion engine

A Benz-Velo used by the publishing firm of Katolik in Beuthen, Upper Silesia, 1896 · Note
the advertisment in Polish and German

WAGEN für Deutsches Kolonialhaus

Bruno Antelmann.

Berlin C. Jerusalemer-Str. 28.

An electric delivery cart in Berlin, about 1900

Above: The "First Karlsruhe Bicycle Club of 1882" sets out for a trip in 1887 on their astonishing twelve-man machine

Below: The first motor lorry with trailers

Below: Werner von Siemens (1816–1892), the great entrepreneur and innovator in electrical engineering, produced his first electric engine to draw a miniature railway at the Berlin Trade Fair of 1879

Benz sports car, 1900 · Behind is a Benz-Comfortable, the 1898 model

23

37 Gustav Krupp von Bohlen und Halbach with his wife, the Krupp heiress, Bertha, at a flying week in Gelsenkirchen, in 1913

Mercedes racing car in the French Grand Prix of 1914

A motor rally at Weimar · Photo: Held

Above: The submarine "Forelle" (Trout) underway on the surface · In 1903, when this picture was taken, submarines were still a novelty

Top right: The submarine "Forelle" being taken by crane to the water at Kiel-Gaarden, in 1903 · The boat was built by the Krupp Germania yard for export to Russia

Bottom right: W. S. Bauer (1822–1875) tests a diving suit he has invented. He was a pioneer in this field, and in the design of submarines

This page:
The departure of the
Hamburg-America
Line passenger liner
"Imperator" from
Hamburg, in 1913 ·
At the time it was
the largest ship
afloat

Page 244: The
"Crystal Palace"
in Munich during
the Industrial
Exhibition of 1854 ·
The picture shows
the interior and
details of the stands

Page 245: A section
of the International
Electrical Exhibition
held at Frankfurt
on Main, in 1891

Page 246: The
Zeppelin "Sachsen"
arriving at Mockau
airport, in 1913 ·
In the background
is the Zeppelin
"Viktoria Luise"

THE EMPEROR AND HIS COURT

The Emperor Wilhelm II was born on January 27, 1859, the first child of Prince Friedrich Wilhelm (nephew of the senile King Friedrich Wilhelm IV of Prussia) and Victoria, Princess Royal of England, eldest daughter of Queen Victoria. As the old King was childless, the baby stood in direct line to the throne, after his grandfather and father. The birth was both difficult and complicated, and such was the relief at the safe delivery of the child that it was several days before anyone noticed that his left arm hung limp and blue from the socket. As a result of this the Emperor's childhood was overshadowed by arduous, painful and often barbaric courses of treatment to remedy this defect, but all to no avail, for the left arm remained several inches shorter than the right, smaller, and almost totally lacking in power. He faced the effects of his disability with a great deal of courage, accepting with fortitude the superiority of other children, especially his younger brother Heinrich, in all normal childhood pursuits. His mother refused to allow him to be treated differently from other children, though it always cost her much to do so, and gradually he came to terms with his difficulties. As a young man he was almost totally physically independent; he learnt to ride, after many initial falls, superbly, to eat with an ingeniously combined knife and fork, and became reputedly one of the best shots in Germany, with a specially designed gun. In pictures the disability is not always apparent, for his uniforms were specially and carefully cut, and he adopted a characteristic pose of resting his left hand on his sword hilt, which minimised the effect of shortness.

His mother had been the Prince Consort's favourite child, and from him she inherited her dazzling intellect, artistic tastes, and passionate love of all branches of knowledge. Endowed with immense energy and her father's sense of duty, she could turn her hand to anything, from politics to planning sewage systems. Unfortunately she could also be impetuous and tactless, antagonising everybody by extolling, as her brother Edward VII observed, the virtues of Britain when in Prussia and those of Prussia when in Britain. Wilhelm inherited many of his mother's mercurial qualities and immense charm, but totally repudiated, to her everlasting sorrow, her liberal views and love of the arts: "This son has never really been mine" she wrote in irritation to Queen Victoria, for whom, in contrast, Wilhelm held a lifelong healthy respect. Mother and son were constantly on bad terms, he often treating her inconsiderately, even cruelly, she always a little too willing to take offence at imagined slights.

Wilhelm succeeded as Emperor in 1888 after the short reign—ninety-nine days—and untimely death of his father, Emperor Friedrich III. He was twenty-nine. In 1881 he had married Princess Augusta Viktoria of Schleswig-Holstein-Sonderburg-Augustenburg, "Dona" to the family. Uncritical, adoring, phlegmatic and uncompromisingly Lutheran in outlook, she was to bear him six sons and a daughter, and represent to the nation as a whole the epitome of the German *Hausfrau*. Where women were concerned, Wilhelm was an ardent upholder of the traditional precepts of *Küche, Kinder, Kranke, Kirche*, and not once in their long marriage was Dona tempted to look beyond these. In the same way as that of Queen Victoria and Prince Albert in England, their ménage set the tone of German society in the late nineteenth century.

As a family they upheld the bourgeois standards of morality, orthodoxy, cosiness and utter respectability, and the thousands of picture postcards sold in Berlin of the Emperor "en famille" bear witness of the popularity of these standards. When Crown Prince Wilhelm reached his late teens, and began to spread his wings a little, his way of life was sufficiently "fast" to add spice and interest without impairing the basic ideals. Though his affairs were talked of all over Berlin, they were known to be fairly innocent. Like his father he married young, and he and Crown Princess Caecilie soon appeared to echo the domestic virtues of his parents.

The court reflected the stolid domestic virtues of the Imperial family; it had none of the glitter of the English court of Edward VII or the dignity of the Austrian court under Franz Joseph. Conscious that Berlin lacked the glamour of London, Vienna or St. Petersburg, it tried to devise a ceremonial which would vie with these older, more established courts. The result, however, appeared contrived and inflexible. The main meal of the day required full evening toilette—uniforms for the men, evening dress with regulation-length trains, long white gloves and fans for the women; this was obviously ideal for an evening dinner in Berlin or Potsdam, but when the Emperor was in Hamburg or at one of his summer palaces, he liked to dine at noon in order to leave the evenings free. Court dinners were always long drawn-out affairs, and the discomfort to the participants, on a stifling summer's day, was considerable. Alcohol was discouraged at these meals; wine and champagne were served but the Emperor and Empress usually drank nothing stronger than fruit juice, and never touched spirits. Nor were after-dinner activities particularly stimulating. No guest or member of the court could retire until the Imperial couple had left and since cards, parlour games or charades, the fashionable evening pursuits of the age, were not indulged in, there was nothing to do except move from group to group and make small talk. Livelier conversation was risky, since the Emperor might suddenly appear at one's elbow and demand to be let in on the joke, and, like his grandmother, he was not always easily amused. "Standing and waiting" said one of the ladies of the court, "that is the chief part of our lives; it makes one mentally and bodily weary until one gets used to it."

Yet the court must have presented a dazzling picture to the outsider, the more so since the colourful and dramatic uniforms of the German regiments were *de rigueur* for anyone who had the slightest right to wear them. The Emperor owned palaces, country houses and hunting lodges all over his considerable empire, from Rominten near the Russian border to the Strassburg Schloss, acquired after the war of 1870-71. His constant urge to move from place to place earned him the nickname of the *Reisekaiser* (Travelling Emperor), but his restlessness meant that a large number of his subjects had a chance to see him and his family in the flesh, which gave a regular boost to the patriotic spirit of the nation.

Wilhelm II honoured Bismarck in retirement with
a visit to his house at Friedrichsruh on the occasion
of his eightieth birthday, on March 26, 1895 ·
Here he greets the ex-Chancellor at the head of his
cavalry detachment of curassiers, whose uniform
Bismarck had himself favoured for formal occasions ·
The thirteen year old Crown Prince stands next to
Bismarck · Although the Emperor and Bismarck
were officially reconciled by this meeting, animosity
still lurked below the surface

The new Emperor visits the old Chancellor at Friedrichsruh on October 30, 1888 · Bismarck
once remarked of his new sovereign "There is a man who will be his own Chancellor" ·
His prophecy came true, for on March 17, 1890, he was forced to resign · The characteristic
upturned moustache which Wilhelm made famous was then in embryonic form

The residence of the Prussian Kings in Berlin – built by
Andreas Schlüter and Johann Friedrich Eosander · In the foreground,
the Schlossplatz with the equestrian statue of the Great Elector

A visit by Wilhelm II to the Czar Alexander Guards Grenadier Regiment at Potsdam,
in 1897 · The regimental mascot, a raven, strides across the parade ground

Wilhelm II and his officers in historical costume · Next to the Emperor is the painter
Adolph von Menzel (1815–1906), whose paintings caught the spirit of Imperial Germany ·
Wilhelm II loved appearing in costume as either Frederick the Great or the Great Elector

A curtsey from students learning domestic science at the Fischbeck Convent, during a visit
by the Imperial couple · The Empress carries a bouquet · The girl in the centre of the picture
is the young Princess Viktoria Luise

Wilhelm II at a reunion-dinner in the Hotel Esplanade in Berlin, 1912

Below: The Kaiser and the Crown Prince on the way to the New Year Parade, 1914 · Photo: Groas

Right: The Imperial pavillion at the opening of the Nord-Ostsee canal, at Altona on the Elbe · Photo: Thiele

The Crown Prince leaving Liebmann's on the Unter den Linden, one of Berlin's smartest
shops and holders of an Imperial Warrant · Next door is the Berlin branch of E. Braun,
Vienna's most exclusive clothing shop

Crown Prince Wilhelm and Crown Princess Caecilie leaving the Marmorpalais in
Potsdam after the baptism of their eldest son in 1906

Below: The Crown Prince at a *concours hippique* in Ruhleben, Berlin, 1911

Right: The Empress and her daughter-in-law Princess August Wilhelm at the spring parade on Tempelhof Field, Berlin on June 14, 1909 · Tempelhof is now the site of West Berlin's main airport

Princess Viktoria Luise (left) and Crown Princess Caecilie (right) as honorary colonels · Viktoria Luise was given her colonelcy of the Death's Head Hussars as a confirmation present by her doting father, Wilhelm II

The marriage of Prince Heinrich of Prussia in Potsdam · He and his bride
are seen inspecting a parade of the First Guards Regiment

Below: The unveiling of the monument to the Emperor Wilhelm I, in Bahrenfeld, 1904 · The Emperor is seen drinking the health of the town of Altona

Right: Crown Prince Wilhelm joins the First Foot Guards at the age of 10, as a first lieutenant · Here, the officers greet their new colleague

Overleaf: Princess Viktoria Luise, the Emperor's only daughter, at her marriage to Prince Ernst August of Hanover · Their marriage ended the feud between the Houses of Hohenzollern and Guelph, which had existed since 1866 when Prussia annexed the Kingdom of Hanover and appropriated the Crown Jewels · It was also the last great gathering of European royalty, with Czar Nicholas II, King George V and Queen Mary, and a host of lesser monarchs attending

THE
GLITTERING
ARMY

The streets of Imperial Germany were often drab and colourless, full of harrassed housewives and pallid business men. Against this neutral backcloth the full splendour of the officers and men of the "glittering army" showed up in startling contrast. Women cleared the pavements to make way for a Prussian officer; even a lowly private walked with a confidence donned only with the uniform. The traditions of the army were Prussian, even, by 1914, in the independent armies of Württemberg and Bavaria. This tradition combined both brutality and progressive thinking. The Prussian drill sergeant was renowned for his ferocity: barbarous punishments could be inflicted on defaulters. Yet the army respected individual initiative. It was not considered enough woodenly to obey orders: officers were taught to use their judgement and even to disobey orders if the circumstances justified it. The iron discipline remained from the armies of King Friedrich Wilhelm I and Frederick the Great, who made the Prussian soldier famous for his skill in battle and solid courage under fire. The imagination came from the reformers, like Scharnhorst and Gneisenau, who had rebuilt the Prussian army from the ruins left by Napoleon after the battle of Jena (1806) and the Treaty of Tilsit. More recently, it had come from the inspired leadership of Helmut von Moltke, whose new style of warfare made the *thinking officer* a necessity if victory was to be achieved. The achievements of 1866 and 1870 came from an army led by a theorist who had never before commanded an army in battle, and as a result the army in the years of peace after 1871 became the most studious in Europe. It was a change strongly resisted by the aristocrats who made up the bulk of the officer corps, but since promotion and success came to depend on knowledge and ability rather than birth, it was in time reluctantly accepted. The General Staff Officer in Germany with the broad red stripe down his trouser-seam, to distinguish him from the mere regimental officer, became the model for all aspiring young lieutenants. By 1914, the Prussian army had managed to combine its gloss and glitter with an efficiency unsurpassed in Europe.

If the intellectual quality of the officer corps had altered, its social character remained the same. Duelling was *de rigueur* and the Courts of Honour enforced the old aristocratic code ruthlessly on errant officers. More and more middle-class officers were appointed, and leavened the aristocratic composition of the army, but they either rose by their merits to staff positions or disappeared to serve in socially undistinguished line regiments. The Guards and the best cavalry regiments like the Death's Head Hussars and the Dragoons remained unsullied by intrusion from the new men. But even the newcomers rapidly adjusted themselves to the traditional standards, collected duelling scars and behaved with the haughty disdain expected of a Prussian officer. For them the army was a road to better things, and they wanted to enjoy the social privileges of the life of a gentleman, not to undermine the established order.

The private soldiers of this model army were drawn by universal conscription from all groups and classes in Germany. The student or middle-class youth with connections could avoid his full period of service and serve for one year as a volunteer. But most served the full three years, later reduced to two. The government looked upon the army as the "school of the nation",

in which such divisive tendencies as voting Social Democrat could be eradicated, and a true patriotism instilled. NCOs were bombarded with pamphlets which told them how to recognise Social Democrats among their men (usually by their "furtive behaviour and surly disposition"). But many people seemed to enjoy their service, and came out the patriots which their superiors had hoped for; the army served the function of drawing the many separate elements of the country together.

One reason for this ready acceptance of military life and duty lies in the attitude of society to the soldier. He was admired, not pitied: "Prussian ladies never tire of watching the soldiers" a Turkish diplomat remarked in 1899. Officers were always obeyed, without question, even by civilians, which gave rise to the classic hoax of the "Hauptmann von Köpenick". A cobbler named Voigt dressed up as an officer, and proceeded to take over the Berlin suburb of Köpenick, since the mayor and all officials accepted him without question.

The army, and later the navy, were the most substantial investment which German state ever made. But it was an investment which paid ample dividends. Heavy industry benefited from the naval building programme. The army provided work in light engineering, in textiles, and a demand for the products of the farmers and landowners of the east. The dependence of society in this economic sphere on an expanding army and navy was recognised by industrialists and even by many politically conscious members of the working class. It helped the glittering army and navy attract support rather than opposition—which foreigners viewed as naked militarism. When it went to war in 1914 the parade dress was put aside for field grey, and by 1918 the army had vanished in the mud of the Western front or in the frozen plains of the East. With it disappeared the core of Imperial Germany.

271

Page 271: The First Foot Guards regimental band marches past the Emperor Wilhelm II on his birthday parade

Right: Recruits being collected from the station in Berlin in 1909 and brought into barracks by NCOs

Above: Parade on Tempelhof Field in Berlin, 1908

Right: The march past of the colour party during
the New Year celebrations in Berlin, 1912

Overleaf: A parade of the Death's Head Hussars · The regiment had close connections with the Royal house: the Crown Prince served in it, and his sister was honorary
colonel · It is interesting to note that all German cavalry regiments carried the lance

The launching of the heavy cruiser "Gneisenau", named after one of Prussia's great military reformers during the Napoleonic Wars, from the Weser shipyard in Bremen, 1896

The launching of S.M.S. "Kaiser Wilhelm II" by the Emperor's brother, Prince
Heinrich of Prussia, at Wilhelmshaven on September 14, 1897

A military sporting competition: a contest in eating bread rolls ·
Even the Prussian army had a sense of humour on occasion

Officers at dancing practice, about 1900 · Every officer who attended a court ball had to
have passed a dancing test conducted under the eagle eye of the court dancing mistress

Das Auswaschen der Handtücher in dem Schwimmbassin ist verboten.

Nicht in das Wasser spucken!

A military swimming bath. The picture has been posed for the photographer · The small notice above the pool forbids spitting in the water

A march-past by the league of veterans (left) and reserve officers (right) · Umbrellas
and walking sticks take the place of sabres · The reserve officer and
the veteran occupied an important place in German society, and promotion was
avidly sought by reserve officers as a mark of official esteem

The changing of the guard, Unter den Linden in Berlin, 1911

Above: The veterans of the First Foot Guards march past the active regiment · Note their smartness, and uniform civilian dress

Overleaf: The First Foot Guards on parade at Potsdam in 1896 · At the end of the file is the fourteen year old Crown Prince

THE CAPITAL CITY

When Wilhelm I was crowned German Emperor, Berlin still had something of the atmosphere of a provincial town. The centre of the city was small, dominated by the Royal palace and the vast and elegant square called the "Forum Fredericianum", with its smaller palaces and public buildings. The most impressive street was the fine avenue called "Unter den Linden", first planted with linden trees by the Dutch wife of the Great Elector. At the end of Unter den Linden was the "Brandenburg Gate", begun in 1793. In 1871, the suburbs of Schöneberg, Friedenau, Wilmersdorf, Charlottenburg, and Westend were still villages, dotted with villas. In the wake of the Franco-Prussian war, the city began to expand, building new streets like the "Kurfürstendamm", Berlin's answer to the Champs Elysees, as well as a rash of badly-built houses and the circle of industrial factories and smaller enterprises which attracted a huge new work force to the city. The old centre of Berlin had been named "Athens on the Spree", for the classical elegance of its buildings: Walter Rathenau with cruel accuracy labelled the new Berlin "Chicago on the Spree". In 1865, the city contained 658,000 inhabitants; by 1875, it had increased to 964,000. By 1910, it had swollen to over two million, and was still expanding at a rapid rate. The old traditional Berlin was swallowed within the new urban mass; the suburbs lost their identity and became dormitories for the workers and middle classes.

Wilhelm II caught the spirit of the new Berlin of which he was the centre. "Berlin is a great city, a world city (perhaps?)... There is nothing in Berlin which can captivate the foreigner, except a few museums, castles and soldiers. After six days, the red book in hand, he has seen everything and he departs relieved, feeling that he has done his duty. The Berliner does not see these things, and he would be very upset were he told about them." It was a gaunt city full of grandiose buildings, like the new Reichstag completed in 1894 and the huge Königs-

platz with its column of victory to celebrate the triumphant conquest of France. Everything in Berlin was on a gigantic scale: *The Times* described the statue of Wilhelm I erected for the centenary of his birth on March 22, 1897. "It is 65½ feet high, mounted on a bronze pedestal, resting on a cruciform block of granite on each end of which lies a couchant lion in bronze. At the front and back of the pedestal are bronze shields bearing the inscriptions respectively 'Wilhelm the Great, German Emperor, King of Prussia, 1861–1888' and 'In gratitude and true affection–the German people.' At each corner stands a winged figure of Victory. On the sides are two allegorical scenes in relief representing war and peace." Much of the pomposity in architecture was due to Wilhelm II, who rejected designs which were not "Imperial" enough. The splendour contrasted with the drab apartment blocks, five or six storeys high, in which most workers lived in discomfort and often squalor.

The Berlin that the foreigner enjoyed most revolved around the great hotels and restaurants. Some, like the Adlon Hotel and Kempinski's Restaurant, had an international reputation; others were known only to Berliners. Food, and more especially drink, was the mainstay of Berlin social life: every Berliner had his preferred "Bierstuben", which the city possessed in abundance. Cuisine was plentiful rather than subtle, a trait which extended to the Imperial court, where long menus, in German, boasted such specialities as "Apple Pei" *(sic)* and "Brot Pudding". But Berlin was an elusive city for the foreigner to appreciate, not merely for its size, but because it was always in a state of flux. The city never settled down, as buildings and monuments only ten or twenty years old were torn down and replaced by new. As the art critic Karl Scheffler wrote, "Berlin was always becoming and never being." It was this restless energy and appetite for novelty which made it a true mirror of the spirit of Germany.

291

Previous spread: The square in front of the Brandenburg Gate with the Reichstag
building behind the trees, in 1899 · Photo: Tietzenthaler

Above: The Schlossplatz with the Arsenal in 1892

Right: Market day at the Gendarmenmarkt, about 1880

The Wintergarden in the Central Hotel · Photo: Schwartz

The Oranienburg Gate · In the background on the right is the entrance to the Borsig heavy-engineering works · Photo: Schwartz

The Potsdam Bridge, seen from
Königin Augusta Strasse, in 1898

Sperlinggasse on the Friedrich canal · Photo: Tietzenthaler, 1909

The River Spree, with the Friedrich Bridge and Emperor Wilhelm Bridge · On the
left bank is the Stock Exchange, on the right the cathedral · Photo: Tietzenthaler

Anhalt station (built 1875–80),
photographed here about 1880–81

Horse-drawn buses in Leipziger Strasse ·
Photo: Tietzenthaler, 1897

Unter den Linden and the
corner of Friedrichstrasse ·
Photo: Missmann, 1909

Left: The Prinzenstrasse stop on the electric overhead railway, about 1900

Below: A sightseeing bus, about 1900 · Photo: Hoffmann

The Sedan Day holiday in the Siegesallee, in 1914, just after the outbreak of war · Sedan Day was always marked by parades and military displays which attracted large audiences · The Siegesallee contained statues of Germany's military heroes in a grandiose style · Photo: Tietzenthaler

11   Trooping the colour, seen from behind the scenes, in Unter den Linden about 1895

The Silver Jubilee of Wilhelm II's accession to the throne in 1888

Left: Pennants bearing the portraits of the Imperial couple were on sale everywhere

Right: A procession of girls crosses the Palace Bridge to pay homage in front of the palace

Left: The high cost of meat · During a meat shortage of 1905, the working classes
could get cheap meat only from the Freibank which sold inferior and sub-standard cuts

Right: The arrival of the "Sachsengänger" at a Berlin station · "Sachsengänger"
were the destitute farm labourers from the east of Germany, who came "West"
at harvest time to find work and better wages · Photo: Haeckel, 1909

The misery of the lower orders: the painter Heinrich Zille has
portrayed their world in a series of photographs

Above: Some of the very poor made a living gathering brushwood and selling
it for use as firewood · Here they drag their waggon over the military exercise ground
in Charlottenburg

Right: The market on Friedrich-Karl-Platz (now called Klausener
Platz) in Charlottenburg

31

Left: Children on the Knobelsdorff Bridge in Charlottenburg, 1900

Above: A family business about 1900: a shoemaker working at home · Many small
businesses were carried on from the overcrowded flats in which most Berlin workers lived

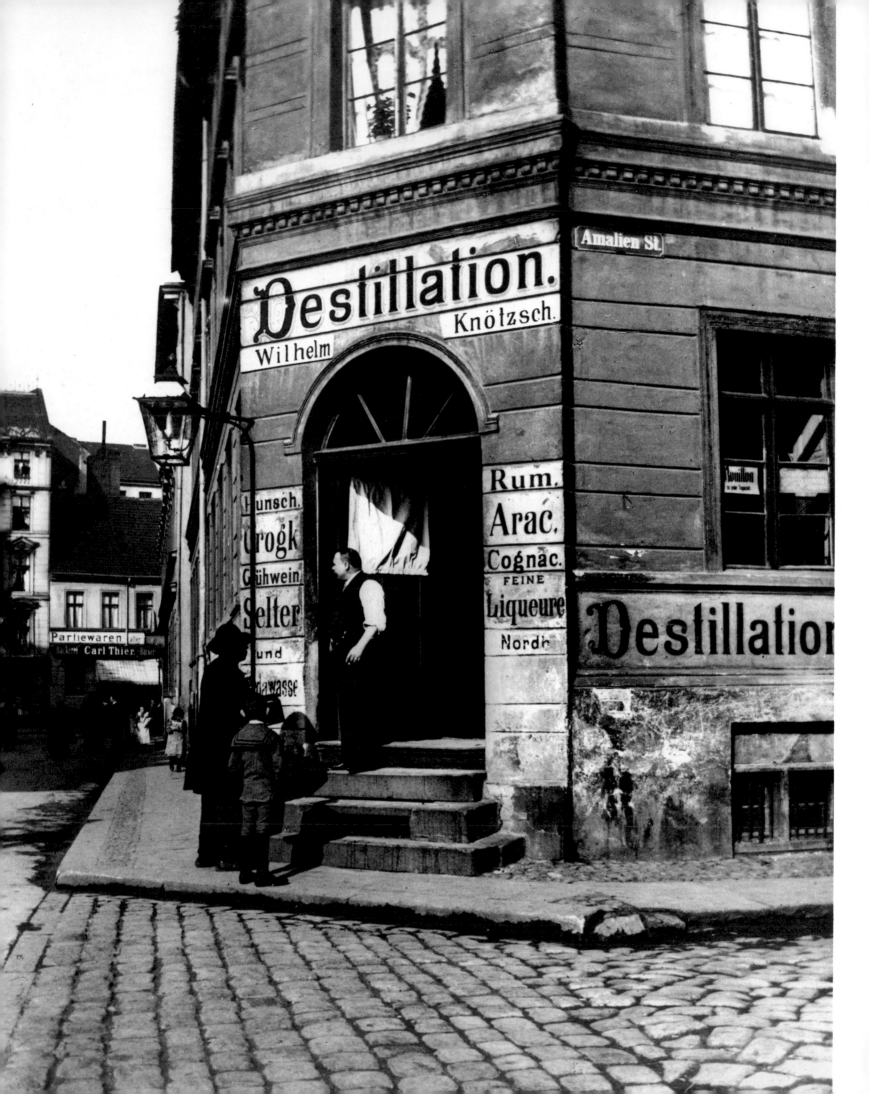

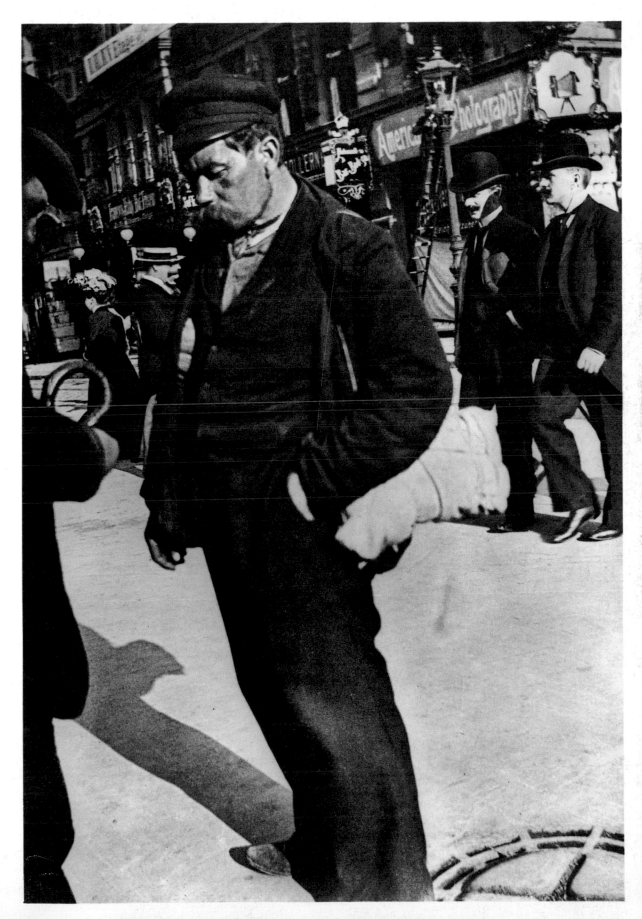

Left: a tavern on the corner of Hirtenstrasse and Amalienstrasse, about 1900

Right: A street scene in Charlottenburg about 1900 · Although a predominantly working-class district, its social composition altered as the city of Berlin expanded to absorb its suburbs

Left: Society ladies "walking out" at the racetrack, about 1903

Below: Nursemaids in the Tiergarten in 1901 · Girls and women from the Spreewald area were much in demand as children's nurses and wet-nurses

The opening of a flower show · Crown Princess Caecilie and her companions
on the way to the opening ceremony

Berlin goes on holiday, about 1905

The corner of Friedrichstrasse and Leipzigstrasse, 1913

Below: A sandwichboard man advertising lunches, in
Unter den Linden, 1900

Right: A procession of the members of the Hotel Keepers'
Association, during an anniversary celebration on
October 14, 1901

Below: The crucial Reichstag election of 1912 · The obedient subject approaches the ballot box

Right: A Social Democrat rally against the three-tier voting structure which existed in Prussia · The orator is Robert Fischer, 1911–12

Overleaf: A press photographer, 1910

A note on the early history of photography

A book of old photographs would not be complete without some comment on the technical developments which made them possible, and the quiet social revolution which the invention and its rapid spread made possible.

Many of the pictures in this book have the caption "daguerreotype", and the inventor of this process, Louis Daguerre, has until recently been looked upon as the undoubted inventor of photography. But in fact credit for the invention must go to another Frenchman. In the small village of Saint-Loup-de-Varennes, a memorial now stands with the words: "In this village, Nicéphore Niepce invented photography in 1822." Today his contribution to the development of photography is acknowledged, although his process was limited in its application. It involved the slow exposure to light in a camera-obscura of glass plates covered with bitumen judaica.

In 1829 Niepce reached an agreement with Daguerre, who had also been experimenting with the camera-obscura, that they should both experiment with techniques for fixing the image produced on the plates, which early experiments had shown to be prone to fading. Daguerre had the greater success, using a chemical formula containing iodine and salts of silver, and after Niepce's death in 1833, he signed a new contract with his partner's son. By this agreement, the process was now called the "daguerreotype". He managed to interest the physicist Arago who in turn acted as Daguerre's advocate with the French government. On his insistence they purchased the rights to the process, and at a historic meeting of the Academy of Sciences on August 19, 1839, details of the invention were announced to the world.

The daguerreotype process produced an image of the highest definition and quality in reverse on a highly-polished silvered metal surface. Because the surface of the plate was like a mirror, the daguerreotype could only be viewed properly under certain lighting conditions. Its main disadvantages, however, were that it was impossible to obtain copies of a daguerreotype and that, despite all the careful experiments, the image still faded in time if exposed to light. The silver surface was delicate and easily scratched. All those drawbacks help to account for the small number of surviving daguerreotypes, and the first chapter of this volume contains some of the finest examples of those which still exist in Germany.

Others were also working, simultaneously, on other photographic processes: Fox Talbot in England, Franz von Kobell, and Karl August von Steinhall of Munich, in Germany. But whereas the two German inventors abandoned their experiments when details of the daguerreotype process were published, Fox Talbot patented his method under the name of Calotype (1841). His process had the immeasurable advantage of working from a paper negative from which copies could be made. The disadvantage was that the image lacked sharpness and definition, because the paper negative could not take so clear an impression as the metal plates of Daguerre, and sharpness was also lost in the copying process. But despite this, Fox Talbot produced masterpieces of photography, although it was the daguerreotype which gained universal acceptance and most of the limelight.

The painter De Laroche, proclaimed after a visit to Daguerre: "From today, painting is dead." Daguerreotype cameras could be found not only in Europe but in America and other parts of the world: Daguerre arranged that apparatus was available from Grioux in Paris, a shrewd and businesslike move. Honours showered down on him, among them an Order of Merit from the King of Prussia. His apparatus was taken up and improved by others. Within three weeks of the announcement in Paris, an optician called Dörffel was experimenting with cameras in Berlin. Immediate experiments began to make the plates more sensitive to light so as to shorten the long exposure times of fifteen to twenty minutes still required. The Professor of Mathematics at Vienna, Pretzel, invented a new portrait lens which made possible the striking portraits seen in this volume. Indeed, the lengthy exposure times may have produced more revealing and interesting pictures for they made it impossible to sustain exaggerated or uncomfortable poses.

In 1851 Archer in England developed the first really practicable system for producing copies of good quality, from glass plates on to paper. This involved the so-called "Wet Collodion" process. The plate was kept in a special sealed case, exposed to light while still wet, and developed immediately after exposure. For the necessary processing, photographers equipped themselves with tents or carts, and the weight of equipment necessary for processing wet-plates outside the studio was well over 100 lb. They were an intrepid and hardy breed.

In 1873, Maddox invented the dry-plate, which did away with all the paraphernalia of portable darkrooms. In 1884 Eastman in the USA produced a rolled paper film for general use, which Steinhal had already worked with, while in 1887 Goodwin, another American, announced a new roll film with a celluloid base. The way to mass production had begun.

With the introduction of cheap and simple film, popular photography became a pastime which swept the world. New industries and inventions appeared to satisfy the demand for new and better photographic equipment. Lenses and camera design improved to such an extent that even fast moving objects could be photographed without distortion. With developments in printing technology, the popular illustrated paper made its appearance, bringing news photographs before an enormous audience. By the turn of the century, the photographic revolution had arrived and was here to stay.

Picture sources

Where a photographer is known by name, this is given in the caption to the photograph.

Staatsbibliothek Berlin/Bildarchiv

20, 25, 33, 38, 58 (2), 84 (2), 110/11, 112, 113, 122, 148, 169, 172, 173, 174/75, 176, 177, 178, 183, 186/87, 190, 191 (2), 192, 196 (2), 197, 201, 202, 204, 206 (2), 215, 250/51, 252, 254, 276/77, 295, 323, 324

Landesbildstelle Berlin

123, 226/27, 260, 280, 282/83, 284, 285, 287, 292/93, 298/99, 300, 301, 302/03, 304, 310, 313, 327, 328, 330, 331, 333

Märkisches Museum, Berlin (DDR)

109, 119, 122/23, 124, 193, 194/95, 274, 286, 296, 297, 305, 306/07, 315

Ullstein Bilderdienst, Berlin

255, 257, 265, 271, 291, 294, 309, 311, 314, 325, 329, Umschlagbild

Stadtmuseum Brunswick

39, 149 (2)

Focke-Museum Bremen

138, 139, 140 (6), 141, 142, 143

Technische Universität Dresden

125, 156/57, 158/59, 160/61, 162, 166, 167, 170 (4), 171

Deutsche Fotothek, Dresden

163, 165

Stadtmuseum Düsseldorf

79

Historisches Museum, Frankfurt on Main

66, 67, 68/69, 70, 71, 72, 73, 74, 75, 184/85, 200, 203, 207, 222, 223

Bavaria Verlag, Gauting near Munich

40/41, 312, 326

Staatliche Landesbildstelle Hamburg

24, 31, 34, 35, 70, 71, 88 (2), 89, 90 (3), 91, 92, 93, 96, 101, 104, 105, 106/07, 108, 114, 115, 118, 120 (2), 121, 126, 127, 162, 164, 168

Museum für Hamburgische Geschichte

29, 94, 95, 97, 98 (2), 99, 100, 102/03, 242/43

Fackelträgerverlag, Hanover

253, 268, 316, 317, 318, 319, 320, 321

Historisches Museum, Hanover

144, 145, 146, 147

Archiv der Stadt Cassel

150, 151

Mittelrheinmuseum Coblenz

22/23, 77, 198/99

Rheinisches Bildarchiv Cologne

80/81, 82, 83

Museum für Geschichte der Stadt Leipzig

152, 153, 154, 155

St. Annenmuseum Lübeck/Fotoarchiv

128, 129, 130/31, 132, 133, 134 (4), 135, 136, 137, 208

Deutsche Schillergesellschaft Marbach

37

Deutsches Museum, Munich

30, 32, 76 (2), 211, 218, 219, 220, 221, 224/25, 228, 229 (2), 230, 231 (2), 232, 233, 234, 235, 236, 238, 240, 241, 244, 245, 246, 308

Stadtmuseum, Munich

26/27, 28, 42, 43, 44, 45, 46, 47, 48, 49, 50, 51, 52 (2), 53, 54, 55, 56/57, 59, 60, 205, 218

Bilderdienst Süddeutscher Verlag, Munich

188/89, 261, 262, 263, 267, 275, 278, 279, 281, 288, 322

Willi Menges, St. Goarshausen

78

Stadtarchiv Stuttgart

21, 36, 61, 62/63, 64, 65

Louis Held, Weimar

239

Historisches Archiv Gute-Hoffnungs-Hütte

85, 86/87, 214, 216/17

Zeitschrift "Daheim"

272/73

Krupparchiv

212/13

Archiv Bodo Herzog

241

Franz Hubmann, Vienna

104, 116/17, 256, 258, 259, 264, 266

I would like to thank the Directors and staff of all the many institutions, together with individuals too numerous to mention, whose friendly help made this volume possible.

Franz Hubmann